Rickshaws, Rajas and Roti

AN INDIA TRAVEL GUIDE AND MEMOIR

REBECCA LIVERMORE

ISBN-13: 978-1543016147
ISBN-10: 1543016146

Copyright

Rickshaws, Rajas and Roti

© 2015 by Rebecca Livermore

Table of Contents

Introduction

INDIA — THE LAND OF RICKSHAWS, RAJAS, ROTI, and more. It's both a wonderful, and in some cases, challenging and stressful country to visit. In spite of some harrowing experiences there, India occupies a place near to my heart.

I wrote this book to help foreign tourists to India have a safe and enjoyable trip that is so wonderful that they'll have a deep desire to return to India, either physically, or through fond memories of the journey. (Let's face it; fond memories are much better than nightmares!)

This book is different than most India travel guides in that while it includes some information on places to stay and things to do and see, it focuses more on how to thoroughly enjoy the trip, how to stay safe, and how to enjoy the deeper cultural aspects of India that may be missed by most tourists.

While practical in nature, it is also part memoir, as sharing my own experiences is one way to help you know what to expect when you make your own visit to India.

Who Should Read This Book

This book is for any foreigner interested in traveling to India, or who wants to "travel" to India without actually leaving home. The stories I share provide a way for you to experience India vicariously, and the practical tips will help you experience India in a safe and enjoyable manner should you ever have an opportunity to experience this great country in person.

Consider this book to be a companion book to books such as Lonely Planet guides. Lonely Planet guides provide the nuts and bolts of travel to India, and this book provides the paint to make them beautiful.

This Book is for You if You:

- Want to travel to India but aren't sure how safe it is (or isn't)
- Plan to travel to India with children, and want to know how to make it an enjoyable and safe experience for them
- Are interested in some of the cultural and religious aspects of India that you may not get in some of the other books on India travel that you read
- Want to know what to eat, what to avoid eating, and how to cook some amazing Indian food yourself in your own kitchen at home
- Need information on how to take care of paperwork, immunizations, and what to pack

In short, it's for any person who isn't from India who wants to travel to India or is interested in India and wants to learn more about it.

A Little about Me

I'm an American who has spent a total of about one year in India, having been there on four different occasions. Info on each of my four visits – that were all very different -- are covered below.

Cultural Researcher

On my first trip to India, I spent a few months there as a cultural researcher. I went there with my husband, and my two children who were 10 and 12 at the time. It was great to experience India as a family, and some of what I share in this book is how to travel to India safely with children.

Being in India as an ethnographer gave me the opportunity to dig deep into the culture, and experience India in a way that few outsiders do. Because of the type of work we did there, we were invited to all kinds of events that most visitors miss such as weddings, baby naming ceremonies, and even a visit to the Jodhpur palace to have brunch with the maharaja.

One of the biggest compliments that I've ever been paid was by one of my Indian friends who stated, "Rebecca, you are totally Indianized." That of course wasn't true, but I appreciated it because it indicated that my attempts to do things, "the Indian way," had not gone unnoticed.

Tourist

On my second trip to India, I went with a friend and former teammate who worked with me as a cultural researcher. We were both missing the Indian friends we made, and India in general, and a short, 2-week visit was in order.

On this trip I experienced India as a tourist, and also fell prey to some of the infamous Indian scams that I had somehow manage to avoid on my first trip. (I'll cover scams and how to avoid them in the first chapter!)

Business Woman

My third trip to India came a few years later, and lasted for six months. My husband and I were interested in the possibility of living in India longer term, and wanted to explore the various business options in India.

Exploring India from a business perspective gave me a different view of India and to deepen my ability to bargain and negotiate.

I also gained a better understanding of what it means to actually live in India as a foreigner, as I had to deal with the mundane aspects of life such as paying the electric bill, and dealing with repairmen for things like broken plumbing.

On this particular trip, our kids once again accompanied us. They were 14 and 16 at the time.

In the end we decided that running a business in India wasn't for us, but it was still a valuable trip as it deepened our understanding of life in India.

We also attended a local Indian church this time, which was something we hadn't previously done.

Speaker at a Christian Conference

My fourth trip to India was the first time I travelled to India completely alone. I went there to speak at a Christian women's conference, and was there for just a week.

During this trip, I found out how little I understood about Christianity in India, even though I'm a Christian and had spent some time in churches in India as mentioned above.

I also experienced one of the most awkward moments of all time, as I made a major blunder in front of an audience. (You can read about that in the Religion section!)

A Note to the Indians (or those of Indian descent) who are reading this book

While my Indian friends told me I was "totally Indianized," I realize that regardless of how "Indianized" I became, I am still, to a large degree, an outsider, and I've written this book fully aware that I'm writing through a lens that is distinctly American. That means that some Indians who read this book may disagree with some of my assumptions and conclusions. If that describes you, in spite of that, I hope that you can, at the very least, understand and appreciate how much I love India, even though it frustrated and perplexed me at times.

For those of you who are of Indian descent, but have been raised in the U.S. or some other country outside of India, I hope that this book gives you a desire to visit the country of your roots, and to enjoy the journey when you do. You have a remarkable heritage that you can be proud of, in spite of some of the less desirable aspects of it.

How this Book is Structured

This book is broken into the following 10 chapters:

#1: The Top Indian Scams and How to Avoid Them

A trip to India wouldn't be complete without being ripped off in some form or fashion, and while maddening, it's seldom dangerous. In this section I tell a story of my own experience with a taxi driver from hell, cover some of the most common scams, and how to avoid them.

#2: Health and Safety

In this section, I cover everything from road safety to health considerations to animal safety issues, to tips for female travelers to India.

#3: Food

I cover various foods you can expect to encounter, food safety issues, my experience with cooking in India, and some Indian recipes you can make at home.

#4: Shopping.

India is a bargain hunter's paradise, with many amazing things you'll want to buy. In this section, I cover the types of things you can buy in India, what to watch out for, and how to get the best price.

#5: Family Life in India

This section is specifically for couples and families traveling to India. In it I cover the things to watch out for, and some cultural considerations to be aware of.

#6: Religion

Religion is an inescapable aspect of life in India. In this section I cover the major religions in India, religious etiquette, and what to expect if you go to India for ministry purposes. I also share some of my own experiences in attending church in India.

#7: Culture

I cover cultural issues in India, how to be polite and avoid offending people, as well as some of the deeper aspects of Indian culture such as arranged marriages.

#8: Holidays

I'm not sure anyone really knows how many gods and goddesses there are in India, but the estimates are at a minimum, several thousand. There are many festivals that are focused on various gods and goddesses, and I cover a few of the main ones. I also cover some of my experiences of attempting to celebrate American holidays while in India, and in one case the mildly disastrous outcome of doing so.

#9: Places to Stay, Things to Do

Unlike many India travel guides, this one is not focused on hotels, restaurants, and so on, but I do cover a few hotels, restaurants, etc. that I personally recommend. The focus in this section is on North India, as that's where I spent most of my time in India.

#10: Masala. Masalas in India are generally mixtures of spices. A little bit of this, and a little bit of that, blended together to give a delicious and distinctive flavor. I called this section, "masala" because it is a hodgepodge section with information that doesn't neatly fit into any of the other sections.

One other thing to note: I have some graphics with text to indicate special areas within the chapters. Those are items such as "True Story," "Kid Tip" and "Recipe." Those are visual markers to help you find those bits and pieces that may be of specific interest to you.

Thank you for joining me on this journey. I'm excited to share it with you!

We've got a lot to cover, so let's go ahead and dive in!

The Top India Scams and How Tourists Can Avoid Them

AFTER NEARLY 48 HOURS WITHOUT SLEEP, my friend Heather and I passed through customs in the Delhi airport and were promptly greeted by numerous "helpful" people who seemed to be on a life or death mission as they competed to be the first to grab our suitcases.

Not taking kindly to having my possessions picked up without my permission, I quickly and forcefully regained control of my luggage and began to scan the airport lobby for the door that would lead outside to the one legitimate prepaid taxi stand.

Having done my research ahead of time, I knew that it should cost me about 250 rupees to get from the airport to my hotel of choice, so I briskly walked past all the taxi drivers calling out prices of 600 rupees or more. What kind of a fool did they think I was? (Don't answer that!)

Finally, an Honest Indian Taxi Driver (Or Not)

"Where are you going, madam?"

"Ashoka Road, near Connaught Place," I replied.

"250 rupees."

Perfect I thought. 250 rupees is exactly what Lonely Planet India said I should pay for the fare. Surely this guy was legit.

It wasn't until Heather and I got into the cab that I remembered the prepaid taxi stand -- the ONE legitimate taxi stand at the Delhi airport that we were supposed to use, and this guy wasn't it. Uh-oh.

Well, how bad can it be? It's one in the morning, we haven't slept for two days, and we just need to get to our hotel, I reasoned. And besides, as we careened wildly out of the Delhi airport parking lot, it was too late to back out.

The "Official" Government of India Tourist Office

"It's like pea soup. I may not be able to drive you all the way to your hotel," the driver informed us shortly after we left the airport.

He had something there. I had checked the weather forecast for Delhi shortly before leaving the U.S. and saw that "smoke" was on the forecast. Not rain, or clouds, but smoke.

SMOKE? What the heck does that mean? I wondered. After arriving, I found that due to the cold weather, all kinds of things were being burned to help people stay warm, so the air was thick with smoke. Add to that the darkness of night, and visibility was indeed poor.

The driver didn't manage to get us to our hotel, but he did manage to get us to a building that had a big sign on the front that indicated it was associated with the Indian government and was the official place to get help as a tourist.

I suppose that should have comforted me, but I had a bad feeling in the pit of my stomach.

I knew that I was being ripped off. . .

AND THERE WAS NOTHING I COULD DO ABOUT IT!

We were promptly greeted as we entered the "official India tourism office."

(An official government building, open at 1:00 a.m.? Hmmm. . .)

"What hotel are you staying at?" the seemingly kind man seated behind the desk asked us.

I gave him the info and he made a phone call. He handed the phone to me, where the man on other end, a supposed employee of the hotel, informed me, "I'm sorry, but since you were so late, we gave your room away. We don't have a room available for you."

At that point, I began to wonder how many people were involved in this elaborate scam to keep me from getting to my hotel.

Not willing to go down without a fight, without permission, I picked up the phone and dialed the number for my hotel. Unfortunately, there must have been some trick to getting an outside line, and I was unsuccessful in my attempt to call the hotel directly.

"Why are you so suspicious?" The man behind the desk asked me.

"This is not my first trip to India," I replied.

"Oh."

We spent that night at an absolute dive at an exorbitant price.

First thing the next morning we checked out of the scam hotel and made our way to the hotel where we initially had reservations. The owner of the hotel confirmed what we already knew; we had been scammed.

India is not only the land of rickshaws, rajas and roti – it's also the land of scams.

The scam that happened to Heather and me is just one of the many that you need to watch out for.

Here are some of the other common scams to be aware of:

Your Hotel is Overbooked

This is the scam that I described above. There are a few variations of it, but the end result is basically the same – to keep you from getting to the hotel you REALLY want to go to, so they can make you stay in the hotel they have some type of agreement with (e.g. get a commission from), which of course will be rundown and overpriced.

Some of the excuses they use will be that they can't find the hotel, or as in my case, the visibility was "like pea soup" so they didn't know if they could get me where I wanted to go.

Here are some tips for avoiding this scam:

#1: When you initially arrive in India, after going through customs, head to a phone and call the hotel where you have reservations. Confirm with them that they have a room reserved for you. This will do two things: (1) It will let you know that you do indeed have a room reserved, in spite of what someone else may tell you and (2) It will let the hotel know you have arrived in country and are on your way.

#2: If arriving in Delhi, be sure to go to the REAL prepaid taxi stand. When you arrive in the Delhi airport, you will see several taxi vendors inside, and there will also be taxi drivers who will approach you and try to get you to go with them.

Ignore all of them, and instead, go outside and to the right, and look for the prepaid taxi stand. Go up to the counter, and let them know where you are going. You will pay them and they will give you a receipt with the taxi number on it. They will also indicate which taxi you are to get into.

One important note here is to NOT give the receipt to the taxi driver until you arrive safely at your hotel. The receipt is how they get paid, and they of course will want to get you to the right place in order to get that receipt.

That [fill in the blank] is Shut Down

Similar to the overbooked hotel scam, this one is where you're told that the place you want to go is either shut down or has moved. And then, of course, they "graciously" offer to take you to a better place.

One place this commonly happens is the New Delhi train station, when you're trying to find the foreign tourist reservations office. Scammers will be on the lookout for people just like you, who are clearly trying to find something, and will let you know that the place is closed, and instead they will take you to a travel office where they get a commission.

I've even had this done to me by men dressed in business attire, who flash an impressive looking badge indicating they are with some sort of official Indian tourist bureau office.

The same basic scam is done for shops you might want to visit, tourist attractions, etc.

If this happens to you, ignore their offers for "help," and keep looking for the right place. If you have trouble finding what you're looking for, approach someone on the street and ask for help. Most likely the people you approach that way will be "regular" Indian people who will be more than happy to help you. A key is that you approach them, rather than the other way around.

Duty-Free Gemstones

If you've ever gotten an email from someone in some African country telling you that some wealthy and important person has died and left a big inheritance that you can claim, so long as you provide bank information and other assistance, you've experienced something similar to the duty-free gemstone scam.

In this scam, a gemstone dealer will approach you, and ask you to deliver gemstones to one of their partners in the U.S. (or your country of residence). The idea is that you buy the gemstones, and then when you deliver them to the partner in the U.S., you are paid a much higher price.

Naturally, there is no partner in the U.S., and you'll just be stuck with the gemstones, which are likely fake.

Having said that, India (Jaipur in particular) is a great place to buy real gemstones for yourself, and I'll cover that in the shopping section.

"Special" Shops

I'll be very surprised if you don't experience this particular scam at least once, particular in large cities such as Delhi.

Here's how it works: You get into a rickshaw and at first it seems that all is well, as the driver heads toward your destination.

All of a sudden, the rickshaw stops – and you're not at the destination. Sometimes there is an awkward moment of silence, before the driver asks you to go into a particular shop – which of course isn't where you want to go.

If you do go in, you will likely see a whole lot of white people, and no Indians shopping there. If that's the case, you likely are in a "special" shop that is a place Indians themselves would never shop. The prices will be much higher, and the shop owners are very high pressure. You may find it very hard to get out of there, and end up spending hours there.

Unless you have a lot of time to burn, and don't mind paying way too much for items, you want to avoid this one.

One tip off that you may be about to be hit with this scam is if the rickshaw fare is much lower than what you would expect. For instance, there may be several rickshaw drivers shouting out fares and one is surprisingly low. You may think you are getting a good deal by taking the low fare, but it's important to know that the rickshaw driver makes up for the low fare by being compensated by the shop owners.

I provide some tips for more legitimate forms of transportation in the Places to Stay, Things to Do section in the chapter titled A Guide to Getting Around Delhi, India. Though I wrote it about Delhi, the information applies to most other cities in India as well.

Being Charged for Photos You Take

India is a GREAT place to take photos. There are so many beautiful and colorful things, not to mention things that make you think, "I'm definitely not in Kansas!" And you do indeed want to take a lot of photos while you are there, when you have an opportunity to do so (I'm not much of a photographer and regret not taking more photos!).

But here's the problem: When you take a photo of certain people (such as holy men) or animals such as elephants or camels that are decorated, you may be expected to pay a tip for doing so.

It isn't a law, but more of an expectation, and you can expect to be yelled at if you don't pay it.

This one may not be a scam as much as it is a cultural thing. The reason I put it under scams is that you likely don't find out that you need to pay for something until after the fact. So the bottom line with this one is to have some change on hand, and know you may be expected to give a tip for some of the photos you take.

"Special" Bracelets

At times you may be approached by either "holy men" or children and have them start to put a bracelet on you that is made of string. They may tell you that it's a gift – but then they expect to be paid for it. If you don't want it, politely decline and stop them from tying the bracelet on you.

Broken Taxi Meters

I provide some transportation tips in the Getting Around Delhi chapter in the Places to Stay and Things to Do section, but I just wanted to mention this issue in the scams section since it's a common one.

Regardless of whether the meter is broken or not, it helps to agree on a price ahead of time. I like to ask an impartial person such as a hotel employee how much it should cost to travel by taxi or rickshaw to a particular location so I have some idea of how much I should pay.

Health and Safety

Health and safety are certainly big concerns in India, much more so than many countries such as the U.S. Naturally, you can get sick or in an accident anywhere, but India seems to be a place with a lot more opportunities for something bad to happen.

That's the bad news. The good news is that you can take certain precautions to stay safe and healthy when in India.

In this chapter I'll cover:

#1: How to Cross the Street in India and Live to Tell About It

#2: Basic Information on Immunizations

#3: Suggestions for Coping with Stress in India

#4: How to Handle (or not!) Wild Animals in India

#5: Tips for Solo Female Travelers to India

#6: Common Diseases

While I cover some of the items in this section, I would also like to recommend that you read The India Travel Health Guide by Shalu Sharma. Shalu is an Indian national that writes a lot of India related travel books.

Unlike some Indians who paint a rosy picture of their country and deny all negatives, Shalu tells it like it is. In fact, I think her book may scare you a bit more than is necessary, but I would still highly recommend it because she provides a lot more food for thought and information on this topic than I can go into in this book.

Now let's get into the meat of this chapter.

How to Cross the Street in India and Live to Tell About It

"Oh God, help me" I uttered, as I took a deep breath and stepped into a small pocket of car-free space on a crowded street in New Delhi. I had been standing on the curb, waiting for a "good opportunity" to cross the street for several minutes when I finally realized that there was no such thing as a good time to cross a busy street in New Delhi.

There were mainly two options: dangerous and less dangerous.

Less dangerous it would have to be.

Since then, I've crossed numerous streets in India, and since I'm writing this book, you can rightly assume that I survived each of my India street crossing experiences. I'd like to let you in on the secrets of crossing streets in India. It can be done!

Secret #1: Look the "Wrong" Way

(This tip is especially for Americans!)

Our mothers taught all of us to look both ways before crossing the street. In spite of our mother's admonition to look both ways, many of us have a tendency to look only the direction that we expect traffic to come.

That works okay when you're the U.S., but since Indians drive on the left side of the road, if you look to your left to see if it's clear like you're accustomed to and then step out into the street, you could lose your life.

In India, it's even more important to look both ways before crossing the street, but if you only look one way, look to your right to see if it's clear before stepping into the street. Remember, if you're an American, it will be the opposite of what you are used to.

Secret #2: Cross the Street When Indians Do

One thing India has is people - lots and lots of people. At times that can be overwhelming, but other times it can contribute to your safety. If you're in a decent sized city in India, chances are, there will be several Indian people who want to cross the street when you do. Don't be afraid to stand close to them, even in the middle of the crowd if possible. Wait for them to start crossing, and then walk when they walk, and stop when they stop.

Not only will they indicate when it's a good time to cross, being one of a crowd increases safety as there is less chance motorists will hit a group of people. If you're in the middle of the group when crossing the street, your safety increases that much more, as the other people shield you from vehicles that come near the group.

Secret #3: Be Prepared to Start and Stop

A reason it took me so long to cross the street in India the first time I needed to do so was because I tried to wait until it was clear enough for me to make it all the way across the street without stopping. In big cities in India, there is seldom a big enough break in the traffic to cross the street safely without stopping somewhere in the middle.

When there is a little bit of an open space, step out and walk a few steps. You may then need to stand there, in the middle of the street for a few seconds, while traffic zips around you. When there is another small break in traffic, walk a few more steps, stopping again when it becomes unsafe to continue walking.

The first couple of times, it may kind of frighten you to be in the middle of the street with cars and scooters zipping around you, but keep in mind that the Indian drivers are accustomed to driving around people, and unless you step right in front of them when they are too close to you to stop, you are really quite safe standing in the middle of an Indian street.

Crossing the street in India can be an exciting experience, but it doesn't have to be life-threatening. Following these tips will help you to safely cross the street in India, should you have the opportunity to visit this amazing country.

Here's a funny video that contrasts driving in the U.S. and India: https://www.youtube.com/watch?v=tPLk9rDl_Wk

This video is actual footage of traffic in India. I chose this one because it's filmed in Jaipur, a city where I lived. I crossed this intersection multiple times and am still alive. https://www.youtube.com/watch?v=pLUm3Q-7iZA

Coping with Stress

India can be an incredibly stressful place, especially for foreigners who are often unaccustomed to all of the sounds, smells, and the multitude of people roaming the streets. Here are a few ways to reduce the stress while traveling in India.

Before you embark on your trip to India, read up as much as possible on the country, so you'll know what to expect. Then, when you see things that are strange and unusual, they are less likely to catch you off guard.

Here are a few ways to prepare yourself in advance for what you'll encounter.

Be Prepared for Traffic

In the U.S. we talk about rush hour and rightly so. But rush hour in every city in the U.S. doesn't compare with the chaos of traffic in India. When I first went to India, it seemed to me that there was no rhyme or reason to the traffic. From what I could tell, there were absolutely no traffic rules, or if there were, no one obeyed them. Over time I began to see that there was at least some system, though it is very different from what I'm accustomed to.

I hope you already read my tips on how to cross the street and live to tell about it. Be sure to revisit that and watch the recommended videos before you go!

Familiarize Yourself with Indian Food

In my opinion, one of the best things about India is the food, but if you're not familiar with it already, all of the options and strong spices may seem a bit overwhelming. Before my family moved to India, I began cooking Indian food at home so we'd be better used to it when we went.

I've included additional information in the Food section of this book on the food you can expect to encounter in India, along with some recipes, which you can enjoy both before and after your trip.

If you're fortunate enough to live near an Indian grocery store where you can purchase some Indian spices, pick up an Indian cookbook or do a search for Indian recipes online, then head to the Indian grocery store to get the ingredients you need. Even a simple trip to an Indian grocery store will give you a little feel for what it's like be in India. If you don't have an Indian grocery store near you, you can order Indian spices online on sites such as Amazon or through a specialty shop such as Savory Spice Shop http://www.savoryspiceshop.com/

If you don't like to cook or don't have time to learn how to prepare Indian food, spend time eating in Indian restaurants. The servers in the restaurant will be more than happy to explain Indian food options to you and answer your questions.

Familiarize Yourself with Indian Culture

Indian culture is vastly different than American culture, so it helps to know the basics before you go. A few things to keep in mind is that the left hand should not be used to give items, particularly food, to people, and shoes should be removed before entering any religious dwellings including Hindu temples, Muslim mosques, and Christian churches. It is also important for women to cover their heads when entering religious buildings or when coming into the presence of dignitaries.

Expect to Get Less Done

As a general rule of thumb, it typically took me at least twice as long to get things done in India as it does in the U.S. In spite of the chaos, when it comes right down to it, things move a lot slower.

If you're an early bird like me, you may be disappointed and frustrated to know that the cities don't wake up too early, at least when it comes to shops and attractions. There are a few exceptions to this (for instance, you want to be at the Taj Mahal at sunrise), but for the most part, things open late.

You can also expect to wait longer for meals to be served in restaurants, to receive your bill, and so on.

None of this is a problem so long as you know ahead of time that everything will take longer than you're used to, and to plan out your days accordingly.

Knowing what to expect and how to behave ahead of time will greatly reduce the stress of traveling in India.

For more information on Indian culture, be sure to check out the Religion and Culture sections in this book.

Animal Safety

In India you'll come across wild animals, even in the city. The most common ones that I've experienced are cows, monkeys, dogs and bats.

Here are a few general tips for when it comes to staying safe around animals in India:

- Most animals will leave you alone if you leave them alone, so leaving them alone is the first tip. Don't do anything to make them feel threatened such as approaching them, or even worse, approaching their young.

- Don't touch or feed animals, no matter how cute they are. You will see some Indian people feeding cows, as they are considered sacred, but I personally advise you not to do so.

- Avoid rodents. That may seem like a "no duh" statement, but in India, there are certain places such as the Karni Mata Temple where rats are considered sacred and are in abundance.

- Avoid wild dogs if at all possible. While it may seem cruel, if you see a pack of wild dogs, pick up a few small stones and toss them toward the dogs if needed. (You don't necessarily need to hit them with the stones, but rather just scare them off. Since you don't want to provoke the dogs, only toss the stones toward them if they start to approach you.)

- If you have any "up close and personal" encounters with animals where your skin has been broken, or you've had contact with an animal's saliva, seek medical attention as soon as possible, just to be on the safe side.

- Be sure to get a rabies vaccination before going to India, particularly if you're going to be in a rural area. I write more about vaccinations in the Diseases chapter in this section.

While all contact with wild animals in India should be avoided, I want to pay special attention to the issue of monkeys, since they seem so cute and lovable.

Beware of Monkeys!

When I lived in India, an American friend of mine there told me that he could always tell how long a westerner had been in India by how he or she felt about monkeys. Those visiting or newly moved to India would exclaim, "Oh, look at that cute little monkey!" but those who had been there for some time would express a different sentiment upon seeing a monkey: "Those filthy creatures!" That was certainly the experience for me. Wild monkeys in India may be cute, but they are anything but sweet and gentle.

According to India Today, Lajpat Nagar, one small neighborhood in New Delhi reported more than 35 monkey attacks on humans in only one month's time. The attacks included bites, breaking into people's homes, and vandalism. It is actually worse in some neighborhoods in Delhi, such as the Yamuna colony of Mayur Vihar, where people arm themselves with sticks, rods, and even firecrackers before they dare to leave their homes. The overpopulation of monkeys is certainly not confined to jungles; Mayur Vihar is referred to as a "concrete jungle" where the majority of people live in apartments made of concrete.

To compound the problem, monkeys often run and attack in packs, making them that much harder to fight off. When one Delhi man came home and found a monkey sitting on his dining room table, he chased the monkey outside, only to encounter and be attacked by five other monkeys. He managed to beat them off, but only after he was bitten several times.

Even worse, according to India Today, in the Kasturba Gandhi Hospital, located near the Jama Masjid neighborhood in north Delhi, monkeys have attacked doctors and have even tried to run off with newborn babies.

Rich, poor, influential people and those who are barely noticed all suffer from the invasion of the monkeys. In fact, according to Yahoo News,in 2007, the deputy mayor of New Delhi was killed when he fell from his balcony while trying to fight off monkeys during an attack.

The cause of the fight between man and monkey is blamed on several factors. First, the monkeys' natural habitat, the Delhi ridge is being depleted, so more monkeys have moved into the city looking for food. Second, many people in India worship Hanuman, the monkey God. As an act of worship, they put out food for monkeys every Tuesday and Thursday, days that are considered sacred for Hanuman. Additionally, garbage filled streets beckon to the monkeys to set up their homes in the city.

India, a country where many animals are considered sacred, is hesitant to kill any animal. In fact, India Today states that the Wildlife Protect Act of 1972 only permits the killing of rats, mice, and the common crow. However, there is a provision that animals may be killed if they are a threat to human life.

In spite of that provision, most Indians will look to another way to control situations such as monkey attacks that have resulted from the overpopulation of monkeys in India.

The bottom line is that when it comes to India, monkeys are here to stay, and while your initial reaction upon seeing them may be, "Look at the cute little monkey!" it's best to have the more jaded approach of, "Those filthy creatures." While cute, it's best to keep your distance from them, and not do anything to provoke them.

I've seen some monkeys react violently to photos being taken – most likely a response to the flash that goes off, so if you want to take photos of monkeys, do so from a bit of a distance, without using flash if possible.

Sources:

India Today: Rage of The Rhesus By Anshul Avijit

http://www.india-today.com/itoday/20010409/monkey.shtml and personal experience and interviews with Indian nationals

My same friend that I mentioned earlier in this chapter on had an interesting experience with monkeys himself. A late sleeper by nature, John was annoyed when a monkey showed up at his apartment at 6:00 in the morning, and started shaking the bars on the window. At first he tried to ignore the monkey, but he kept making a racket while John was trying to sleep.

Irritated as a result of being awakened by the pesky monkey, John got a spray bottle full of water, and started to spritz the monkey with water, in hopes that it would make the monkey go away.

The monkey did go away, only to return with friends. From that day on, for several days (if not weeks) every morning before dawn, five or six monkeys showed up at John's apartment, and shook the bars on his window.

I think he may have been better off ignoring the first monkey, who perhaps would have been bored and found another poor soul to harass.

I never had such a dramatic experience with monkeys, though they did sometimes startle me when they seemed to appear from out of nowhere and run straight at me. Since they kind of freaked me out, I tended to keep my distance, so other than having some buttons pulled off my clothes that were hung out to dry, the monkeys never did too much to me.

Tips for Solo Female Travelers to India

(Side note: Many of these tips are good for women traveling to India, whether alone or not, so even if you're going with a group, with a spouse, etc. it's be a good idea to read this chapter.)

India is an interesting place as far as women are concerned. Mothers seem to be respected, but many other women are not, and foreign women are viewed differently than nationals, meaning that it's assumed that foreign (western in particular) women have loose morals, and because of it, they may be subjected to unwanted advances.

The thing that can be challenging is that the rules for women in India are different than rules for women in the West, so if they're not careful, women who travel alone may inadvertently put themselves in danger.

Here are some safety tips for women traveling to India.

Join a Group

Just because you travel alone to India, doesn't mean you have to see the sights alone. If possible, join a group tour. This is especially important when going to more remote places, where you might be isolated if alone.

Stay in a Guest House

Guest houses, similar to American bed and breakfasts, are a great option for solo female travelers to India. The thing that makes guest houses especially good for female travelers is that the hosts of the guest houses take a specific interest in their guests and may escort them various places, or arrange for tours and transportation options with well-respected and reliable companies.

Guest houses are also a great way to enjoy meals with others in a safe and comfortable setting.

Breakfast is generally included, and sometimes even dinner is a family affair. This is not only safe, but provides a great way to get a glimpse into the life of an Indian family and to meet other travelers.

I personally recommend Rajputana Discovery. I was well looked after by the hosts, and also saw how they took care of other guests, including females traveling alone. I'll provide more information on them in the Places to Stay, Things to Do section of this book.

Dress Modestly

Modesty is incredibly important for female travelers to India. The difficulty is that modesty by Western standards and modesty by Indian standards are two very different things.

Here are a few things to keep in mind, when it comes to modest dress in India:

> •Avoid showing your legs and even your ankles. Capris may be seen as very modest in the West, but would be rather scandalous in India. Bare midriffs, on the other hand, are fine!

•Do not wear sleeveless tops. It may be very hot when you are in India, but avoid the temptation to throw on a tank top, and definitely do not wear something like a halter top. Even cap sleeves are a bit too daring. If it's hot, rather than wearing skimpy clothing, try wearing loose-fitting, lightweight cotton clothing.

•Wear loose-fitting clothing. Loose fitting clothing isn't just good because it's easier to stay cool when wearing it, it can also be considered more modest. Jeans may seem modest to you, but since they are often tight-fitting, they are not considered modest there. If you do wear jeans, wear a long, loose-fitting blouse with them.

•If you have an opportunity to do so, purchase a couple of sets of Indian outfits, known as salwar kameez. These are more comfortable and easier to wear than a sari. You can purchase them inexpensively in India, or if you want to get some before you leave for your trip, check out the selection on eBay.

- •Have a scarf on hand to cover your head when appropriate. This tip may not be as essential as the others, but Indian people really appreciate it when a western woman covers her head in religious buildings such as mosques and temples and when in the presence of elders and dignitaries.

The bottom line is that women can indeed travel safely in India, so long as the culture is understood and right precautions are taken.

Diseases

Obviously, diseases abound in every country, but there are certain diseases that are fairly common in India, that are less common in other parts of the world such as the U.S., Canada and Europe.

The only disease I'm going to cover here in this book is malaria, because it's the one I'm most familiar with, and I've made a point of writing from experience, rather than research alone in this book.

If you want more information on diseases in India, I recommended reading Shalu Sharma's book, The India Travel Health Guide.

Also, be sure to get the proper immunizations before going. Rather than list them here, I'd prefer to refer you to the India information on the Center for Disease Control website, which you can find here:

http://wwwnc.cdc.gov/travel/destinations/traveler/none/india.

This is important because certain diseases that are prevalent today, may be less prevalent when you go, and ones that were not a concern for me when I was there, may be a big problem now. Because of this, you always want to base your immunization decisions on current information, rather than on information that may be outdated.

If you reside in the U.S., you can also consult with your local health department, which is where a lot of my colleagues got their immunizations. In most cases, the health department will be up on what immunizations you need, but in case the one you visit has a low volume of people traveling to India, it doesn't hurt to print off the information from the Center for Disease Control website and bring it with you.

I and my family got our immunizations on base, at military clinics and hospitals, since my husband is retired Army. If you are military, or a military dependent, check with the local military hospital or clinic to see what they have to offer. Chances are, the clinic already has your medical records, and it can be helpful to keep all your records in one place. On top of that, unless military health benefits change, you won't have to pay anything for medications and immunizations you receive on base, so you may as well take advantage of the benefits!

One key thing to keep in mind is that is that it's extremely important to get your immunizations at least a couple of months before you plan to go to India because some immunizations have to be administered more than once to be effective. Again, do your research as early as possible before planning your trip. You definitely don't want to put this off until a week before you go!

Malaria

One fairly common disease in India is malaria. It is common enough in some areas that many of the people who reside there have had it multiple times. Malaria is not so common in the U.S. and other western countries, which is a good thing, of course.

However, the flip side of this is that travelers who contact malaria when traveling abroad in countries such as India may not have any symptoms until they return home. Doctors in the U.S. and other countries where malaria is less common may not immediately diagnose malaria, since they are less familiar with it.

Therefore, it is important for travelers who go abroad where malaria is more common to educate themselves about the symptoms of malaria so they can get treatment when needed, sooner rather than later.

Take Necessary Precautions to Prevent Malaria When Traveling Abroad

Before I get into the symptoms of malaria, I think it's important to cover how to avoid getting malaria in the first place.

The main way to prevent malaria is to take anti-malarial medication while traveling in areas where malaria is common. The Centers for Disease Control and Prevention provides a list of drugs which can be used to prevent malaria, along with considerations such as the side effects of the drugs.

It's important to note that the drugs do not themselves prevent a person from getting malaria, but rather they fight off the disease as soon as it is contracted. Most likely, people who take anti-malarial medication will not even know if they've contracted malaria, due to the action the medication takes against the disease.

Since malaria is spread by mosquitoes, in addition to taking anti-malarial medication, those who travel abroad can protect themselves from contracting malaria by avoiding mosquito bites. That can be done by wearing long pants or skirts and long-sleeved shirts or blouses. Mosquito repellant can also be used, and it's also a good idea to use a mosquito net when sleeping.

If you've done all of the above to prevent malaria, chances are slim that you'll get it. However, if you get any of the symptoms of malaria, it's important to get medical attention as quickly as possible.

Symptoms of Malaria

Symptoms of malaria include:

- •Abdominal, muscle, or back pain
- •Chills and sweats
- •Headache
- •Vomiting or nausea
- •Fever
- •Coughing
- •Lack of energy
- •Diarrhea

The symptoms of malaria are often manifested between seven and 12 days after infection occurs.

The difficulty with the symptoms of malaria is that so many illnesses cause these same symptoms. That is that much more reason why it's important to let a doctor know if you've been traveling abroad if you have such symptoms after returning home from your trip.

Food

Although my skin is fair and I live in the western hemisphere, and although I grew up on bland meat and potatoes, in my opinion, the food is one of the things I love most about India. Here's why:

#1: Indian food is spicy.

Not all Indian food is spicy in a hot sort of way, but it is all flavored with numerous spices. The spices cause even the most humble food, such as lentils, to come alive with magnificent bursts of flavor.

#2: Indian food is, for the most part, healthy.

Although some Indian food is cooked with more oil than ideal, most Indian food (except for desserts) is created with healthy ingredients such as vegetables, spices, and legumes. When I eat Indian food, chances are I'm eating food that is not only pleasing to the pallet, but good for my body as well.

#3: Indian spices makes vegetables that I and my children dislike taste good.

For instance, my family cannot stand eggplant, but when we lived in India, we gladly ate it. Prepared properly and seasoned well, eggplant and other less popular vegetables are delicious. (The only exception to this for my entire family is bitter melon. No matter how it is prepared, we detest bitter melon! Consider this a warning: stay away from the bitter melon!)

#4: Indian food is great for vegetarians.

A good percentage of Indians are vegetarians and thus they have great experience with knowing how to best prepare a great variety of vegetarian dishes. Although I do eat meat, I barely missed meat when living in India, due to the excellent variety of Indian vegetarian food.

Also good to note here is that if you are served some type of food and you don't know what it is, the good news is that due to the high percentage of vegetarians, chances are, the mystery food is some type of vegetable. It would be highly unlikely for it to be some type of "exotic" (and disgusting) animal or insect.

#5: Indian food includes great breads.

I love the variety of Indian breads, which include mostly flatbreads such as naan and chapattis. Nothing beats the slightly smoky taste of naan, fresh out of a clay, tandoori oven, and chapattis are a great way to include complex carbohydrates into your diet.

#6: Indian food is inexpensive.

There may be exceptions, but most Indian food is created with simple ingredients such as vegetables and legumes. The only exception is that numerous spices are used in Indian food and spices can be expensive --- if you're preparing Indian food in your home country. However, spices, when purchased in Indian grocery stores, are very reasonably priced.

Notice that I mentioned preparing Indian food in your home country. If you're like me, when you return to the U.S. (or wherever you are from), one of the things you'll miss the most about India is the food!

While Indian restaurants in the U.S. are OK, after experiencing the real thing in India, I've found the best way to get anything close to that is to cook it yourself.

Lucky for me, I had the best teacher, our family's cook, Chandu, to teach me to cook Indian food.

I Fell in Love with Cooking in a Kitchen in India

"Madam, come cook." As I looked up, I saw Chandu, my Indian cook, smiling at me, with a spoon in his hand. Hearing the words, "Madam, come cook," had become part of my daily routine, and I welcomed the opportunity to learn how to cook Indian food from a man who grew up cooking chapattis and spiced lentils over an open fire in the village where he was raised.

As I mentioned previously, my husband and I, along with our two children, had moved to India to explore business opportunities.

One of the perks of living in India was having household help, including a cook.

At the beginning I was content to let Chandu do all of the cooking, but I knew that when I returned to the U.S., Chandu wouldn't move with us. If I wanted to continue to enjoy home-cooked Indian food at home, I was going to have to learn how to cook it myself.

It all started with bell peppers, stuffed with spiced potatoes, then charred in a cast iron skillet. The moment I took my first bite, I knew I just had to learn how to make them. They were that good.

"Chandu, can you teach me how to make this?" I asked, and he happily agreed. The next time he made potato stuffed peppers, he called me into the kitchen so I could watch him prepare them.

Chandu continued to impress me with the variety of recipes he knew off the top of his head. I never saw him refer to a cookbook or recipe of any kind, and yet he never made the same thing twice, unless we specifically requested some of our favorite dishes. The more Chandu cooked for us, the more I wanted to learn, until I eventually spent every evening in the kitchen with him, with a notebook and pen in hand.

After we returned to the U.S., armed with my notebook filled with Chandu's recipes and an assortment of Indian spices and ingredients, I set out to see if I could replicate the recipes Chandu prepared for us.

That was over ten years ago, and I still cook Indian food at home on a regular basis.

Here's the recipe that started it all:

Chandu's Indian Potato-Stuffed Bell Peppers

3 medium potatoes, peeled and cut into large chunks

1 cup chopped cilantro

2 teaspoons amchur (dried mango powder) or 2 tablespoons lemon juice

1 teaspoon salt

1 teaspoon pepper

1 jalapeno pepper, chopped

¼ cup butter, melted

¼ cup milk

4 green bell peppers

2 tablespoons oil

2 teaspoons cumin seeds

1 cup water

Boil the potatoes until tender. Drain and then mash the potatoes, mixing in the cilantro, amchur or lemon juice, salt, pepper, jalapeno, butter and milk. Set aside.

Trim the base of the bell peppers so they stand flat. Slice off the tops of the peppers and remove the seeds and the white pith. Reserve the tops of the peppers for later use.

Fill each pepper with equal amounts of the spicy potato mixture and replace the pepper tops.

Heat the oil over medium high heat in a pot that is deeper than the height of the peppers. Cast iron works best, but any pot that is deep enough will do.

When the oil is hot, toss in the cumin seeds, stir, and cook until the seeds sizzle and turn a brownish-red color. This should take about 30 seconds.

Stir the water into the pot and carefully place the stuffed peppers into the pot.

Cover the pot and cook until the peppers are tender, the water is absorbed, and the bottoms of the peppers are slightly charred.

For those who never have a chance to LIVE in India. . .

Okay, most likely you won't have a chance to actually live in India, and therefore won't be able to hire your own cook, and will buy food in restaurants, and if you dare, from street vendors. (More on that in a minute!)

Here are some of the foods you can expect to come across on your trip to India.

Common Indian Food Options

"What's aloo paratha?" my son asked. "I don't know. Order it and we'll find out" I replied. And so began our journey into the wonders of Indian food.

Especially when we first arrived in India, in spite of the fact that I had prepared a fair amount of Indian food at home prior to our visit, for the most part, the items on menus in Indian restaurants were quite a mystery to us!

Thankfully, we're pretty adventurous eaters, so our common practice was for each of us to order a different dish, and then we all shared whatever we ended up with. Through trial and error, we learned what foods we liked and which ones to avoid and we also learned the Hindi words for most Indian foods.

The most important lesson we quickly learned was that we simply couldn't go wrong if we ordered any type of Indian flatbread. This served us well because as long as we ordered plenty of bread, we knew we'd walk away from the table deeply satisfied.

Come along with me as I share my love of Indian flatbreads with you. (Later in this chapter I'll go over some of the other common food options. I just had to start with bread because it is SO delicious.)

Characteristics of Indian Flatbread

Indian bread is quite different from what we often think of as bread in the western world. As you no doubt gathered, Indian bread is most often, well, flat. Many Indian kitchens do not have ovens, so most bread is made on the stove-top. An exception is naan, which is made in a tandoor oven, but is still flat.

In my experience, the most common Indian flatbread is the humble chapatti. A chapatti is made with whole wheat flour, salt, and water. After kneading, it is rolled out thin, like a tortilla, and cooked on a metal (often iron) pan, on the stove top. After cooking on the pan, the chapatti is then place directly on the flame to puff. The chapatti is eaten by rich and poor, high-caste and low-caste alike.

Most Indian flatbread is made with whole wheat flour, though some, such as naan, are made with white flour. Naan is one of the few Indian breads made with yeast. Some Indian breads are stuffed with savory food items such as a mixture of potatoes, cilantro, and onions. Others are deep fried. All are delicious.

How I Make "Naan" at Home

(Not 100% authentic, but pretty darn good!)

Naan, particularly garlic naan, is my favorite Indian flatbread. After returning to the U.S., I largely mastered Indian cooking, primarily through following recipes in Indian cookbooks. My friends and family all raved over my Indian cooking, but there was one thing I simply could not do: make naan.

The problem is, naan is traditionally cooked at 900 degrees Fahrenheit in a clay oven, called a tandoor. Even most Indian families do not have a tandoor, and at a few thousand dollars, not to mention having no idea where in my kitchen I would put one, I certainly didn't foresee buying one any time soon. So I regularly cooked Indian food at home, and when we just couldn't stand not having naan, we'd head to the nearest Indian restaurant, where naan was sure to be served.

Being the frugal person I am, I tried to cook naan. I tried every recipe I could find. Every now and then I'd get renewed hope when I came across a new recipe or method for cooking naan, but they were always dismal failures. Sure, they tasted okay. Tasty even. But they weren't naan.

One thing all the recipes had in common was they required the use of an oven at a high temperature. That makes sense, because naan is indeed usually cooked in an oven. So imagine my skepticism when I found a recipe where the naan was not cooked in the oven, but on the stove top. In a cast iron griddle. With a lid (which would simulate an oven). I got up my nerve to give it a try.

Oh my. It was good. Really good. Did it turn out 100% like naan I would get in an Indian restaurant? Not quite. But pretty darn close. So close in fact that I now cook naan regularly at home, and we are no longer overly impressed with naan purchased in Indian restaurants.

Come along as I show you how to cook naan in a simple cast iron griddle, on the top of your stove.

Note: You can use whatever naan recipe you like. I'm going to give you my easy recipe for naan dough, but if you already have a favorite naan recipe you love, feel free to use it. In my estimation, the cooking method is far more important than the actual recipe you use.

#1: Start Off With Yeast, Salt and Garlic Powder

Measure 3/4 tablespoon of yeast, 3/4 tablespoon of salt, and 1 teaspoon of garlic powder into a bowl.

#2: Add yeast, salt and garlic powder to water

Pour two cups of warm (body temperature) water into a large mixing bowl. Dump in the yeast, salt and garlic powder. Don't worry about whether or not the yeast dissolves, and don't wait for it to proof. Just stir it a bit.

#3: Stir in Flour

Dump 3 cups of flour into the bowl and stir. Just stir until the ingredients are mixed. No need to over do it!

#4: Let the Naan Dough Rise

Loosely cover the dough and set it aside to rise for about two hours. The best way to cover the dough is to simply place a lid on top of it, but don't snap the lid in place.

#5: Heat the Cast-Iron Griddle

A secret to cooking naan on the stove top is to get the cast iron griddle good and hot. I've found that on my stove, that takes about 4 minutes, at medium high heat. You may need to experiment a bit with your stove to find the perfect setting. Until I figured out the timing with my stove, the first piece of naan didn't turn out perfectly, but the rest of the batch was great.

#6: Start With Enough Dough to Make One Large Naan

While your cast-iron griddle is heating, pull off a blob of dough, about the size of a small peach. If you're using the cast iron griddle I recommend, you don't want to go too huge or when rolled out, the dough won't fit into the pan. (Notice that I placed the dough on a floured surface. The dough may be a bit sticky, so have some extra flour handy.)

#7: Roll Out the Dough for Naan

Naan is traditionally tear-drop shaped. I used to worry about the shape, but I no longer do. The reason is that since my family loves naan so much, when I cook it, I make a lot. And I currently only have one cast iron griddle, so it takes a lot of time. My objective therefore is to roll out the dough in a shape and size that almost covers the griddle.

The main thing is to roll out the dough until it is about 1/4" thick, or even a little thinner than that.

Don't agonize over this step. The shape really doesn't matter. Naan tastes so good, no one is going to care how it is shaped!

#8: Place the Dough on the Heated Griddle

Spread about a tablespoon of ghee (clarified butter that you buy at Indian grocery stores) on the hot griddle. If you don't have ghee, use a tablespoon of oil, or half oil and half butter or margarine. It all works fine, though ghee is more authentic.

Place the rolled out naan dough onto the hot griddle and cover with a lid.

(The griddle doesn't come with a lid, so just grab any lid in your kitchen that seems to be the right size. I like using one that is clear so I can see how the naan is coming along. The one I use is also nicely domed, so there is plenty of room for the dough to puff up.)

#9: Create a Stove-Top Oven

Putting a lid on top of the griddle is what allows the naan to "bake" on the stove-top. You don't want to just fry the bread, you want to bake it, so be sure to use a lid!

#10: The Dough Will Begin to Puff Up

Large air bubbles are a good sign! This means your naan is cooking as it should. This generally takes a couple of minutes.

#11: Flip the Naan Over

When the naan is nicely browned, lift it up with a spatula and spread about a half a tablespoon of ghee or the butter and oil mixture on the griddle. Flip the naan over, and cover the pan again with a lid.

#12: Cook Until Browned on the Bottom

Cook for about two minutes, until the naan is nicely browned on the bottom. Don't worry about it if you have a couple of burned spots. That actually adds to the smoky taste often associated with tandoori naan

Note: Since you'll cook your naan on a very hot cast-iron griddle, it may get smoky. You'll probably want to run the fan on your stove and/or open your kitchen window to avoid setting off the smoke alarm!

#13: Spread the Naan with Butter if Desired

You may or may not want additional butter at this point. If you do, I recommend a silicone pastry brush. It's a lot easier to clean than the old-fashioned pastry brushes.

Hint: if you didn't put garlic in the dough and want garlic naan, you may sprinkle a bit of garlic salt onto the buttered naan at this point. This is a great option for times when some people want garlic and some don't. If the opinions on garlic are mixed, make the dough without garlic, and add it to just some of the completed naan.

Other Common Foods in India

Below is a list of some of the most common foods you'll come across in India. One important note is that since there are multiple languages in India, the same foods are often called by different names.

To complicate matters, since Indian languages don't have Roman alphabets, when the words are Romanized, they often have different spellings -- sometimes even on the same menu. For instance, you may see aloo or alu on a menu, and they both mean the same thing.

Also, you'll find that many dishes such as vegetables are mixed, so you'll see the names of two vegetables together. For example, you may see "gobi aloo" on a menu. Gobi is cauliflower and aloo is potato, therefore "gobi aloo" is a vegetable dish that consists of both cauliflower and potatoes.

When possible (meaning when I know multiple words!), I've put the word that I'm most familiar with first, and then indicated when it also goes by another name.

This list is by no means exhaustive, but hopefully it will give you at least some clue what you're about to order.

If you're traveling with at least one other person, I recommend doing what our family did and have each person order something different, then eat it family style. That way you get to try a lot of different foods which makes it easier to discover foods you like. You can always order more of something that really hits the spot!

Aloo -- Potatoes

Baigan -- Eggplant

Bindhi -- Okra

Biryani -- a main dish made with rice. Can be vegetarian or not

Chana -- Chickpeas or garbanzo beans

Chapatti -- Flat bread made with whole wheat flour, similar to a non-fat, whole wheat tortilla

Dal -- the general word for legumes

Dosa -- It will be hard not to be impressed the first time you see a dosa. Basically, it's a paper-thin pancake-like "wrapper" that is stuff with a spiced potato mixture. I can't do it justice by trying to explain it, so you simply have to order one when you have a chance!

Kheer --This is essentially rice pudding -- sometimes has nuts and is flavored with cardamom. Side note on this: I have no idea why, but I've had at least one Indian person be incredibly insulted over the idea that kheer is rice pudding. She was insistent it is NOT rice pudding. But it's rice, cooked with milk and sugar until it becomes thick and pudding like. Call it pudding at your own risk!

Makhani -- With butter. For instance, you will see dal makhani on menus, and that means dal with butter, because butter is added at the end of the cooking time. Another popular item is called "Murgh Makhani" which is butter chicken. If you have a chance to eat butter chicken, go for it! (Just trust me on that one!)

A funny "makhani story" -- The first time we went to India, our entire group did a lot of walking. We didn't have cars, and while we took a lot of transportation such as rickshaws, the amount of walking we did resulted in everyone in our group losing weight. Everyone, that is, except my husband. We couldn't figure out why everyone else was losing weight and he wasn't, until we found out what makhani really means. The situation was that early on he discovered dal makhani, and loved it, so he ate it almost every day, not realizing he was eating food drenched with butter and loaded with calories! So if you're trying to watch your calories, skip menu items that include the word, "makhani."

Matar -- Peas

Murgh -- Chicken

Naan -- Flatbread made with white flour and yeast and cooked in a tandoor (clay) oven

Numkeen -- The broad word for snacks.

Paneer -- Referred to as "cottage cheese" but it's nothing like cottage cheese in the U.S. It's a very light, mild cheese, with the texture of tofu. If you find little "white cubes of something" in a sauce or in with a vegetable such as spinach, chances are it's paneer.

Poha -- Flattened rice. This stuff kind of reminds me of Rice Krispies cereal -- except you DON'T pour milk over it and eat it with a spoon. It can be cooked with spices and vegetables and served for breakfast, or can be used as part of a snack mix. For instance, sometimes you find numkeen (see above) made with poha as one of the ingredients.

Rajma -- Kidney beans

Roti -- The broad word for bread -- it refers to all types of breads

Saag (also known as palak)-- Spinach

Tikka -- Boneless -- okay, let me admit that I'm not sure that the word Tikka REALLY means boneless because you'll see things like paneer tikka -- and paneer (see above) doesn't have bones no matter how you slice it! But if you see something like Chicken Tikka on a menu, it means that the chicken is boneless.

I'm well aware that I only scratched the surface of the food items you'll see menus in Indian restaurants, but at least you'll know more than I did when I first landed.

Indian Street Food

Street food is simply food that is prepared, sold and served along the side of a road, or on the street, and thus has become known as street food. It is often cooked and served from portable stalls. Street food is common in many countries, including India.

Indian street food is something that foreign travelers to India shouldn't miss, for several reasons -- so long as they take necessary precautions.

Here's why you should consider giving street food a try. First of all, street food is simply a way of life in India, and partaking of it is a great way to experience a bit of Indian life in the same way that the locals do.

Secondly, Indian street food is delicious, and easy to find. Simply walk up any busy street in India (as well as some not so busy ones) and you'll be sure to find local vendors cooking up delicious food.

Finally, Indian street food is very inexpensive, and so it's a great thing for budget travelers, or anyone who wants to tight-wad on a meal here or there.

Read on to learn about common Indian street foods and how to stay safe while buying food from street vendors in India.

Some Popular Indian Street Food

Pakora: Vegetables that have been dipped in a batter made with chickpea flour, and deep fried. Pakora is often served with cilantro chutney.

Dosas: As mentioned above, dosas are a very thin, crepe-like pancake that are stuffed with a spicy potato mixture.

Samosas: Samosas are pastries that are stuffed with vegetables, dal or in some cases meat. They are shaped like a cone, and as is the case with a lot of Indian street food, deep fried.

Jalebis: Jalebis are deep fried, Indian sweets. From a looks perspective, they remind me of funnel cakes, but have a distinctly Indian taste.

Indian Street Food Safety

Although Indian street food is delicious and inexpensive, there is a downside: you might get sick eating it. Fortunately, India is cracking down on hygiene when it comes to Indian street food, but the standards are still often not quite up to snuff from a western perspective. Therefore, it is important to take care when eating street food in India.

Here are a few tips for eating Indian food without developing tummy troubles:

• Choose to eat at places that are busy. If Indian people are lining up to buy the street food, chances are it is good. Still, the Indian stomach may be more used to eating such foods, so a crowded stall, though a good sign, is only the first thing to consider.

•Pay more attention to the cooks, than to the condition of the stall. For instance, the stall may be pretty battered and worn by American standards, so don't be put off by the looks of the stall itself. Instead, pay close attention to the cooks. Their clothing should be relatively clean. It may be spattered with food, but shouldn't be otherwise dirty.

•Take a look at the cook's fingernails. Clean fingernails are a sign of good hygiene, and since they are handling the food with their bare hands, you want to make sure to purchase the food from a street vendor who has taken care to wash his hands, and cleaned his nails.

How to Make Indian Pakora

Pakora is a popular food that can be purchased from Indian street vendors, and is also a popular snack served in restaurants and homes. The great news is, it is easy to make pakora at home, particularly if you have a deep fryer.

Pakora starts with a batter, made from chickpea flour, also known as besan. Regardless of the type of pakora you make, you will always start with the same batter.

Here is a great and easy recipe for pakora batter:

1 cup chickpea flour (besan)

3 tsp oil

1 tsp. ground cumin,

1 ½ tsp salt

½ tsp. ajwain seeds (optional)

1 chopped jalapeno pepper

1 cup water

Mix all of the ingredients for the pakora batter together in a blender for about five minutes. Although the ingredients will be well blended before then, beating them for five minutes will make the batter light and fluffy.

Set the batter aside for 30 minutes.

While the batter is resting, prepare the vegetables.

The vegetables you use depend on personal taste, but some common ones are cauliflower, cut into small florets, sliced potatoes, and sliced onions.

One delicious option is to prepare a combination of vegetables and create a mixed vegetable pakora.

Mixed Vegetable Pakora

1 small cauliflower, cut into small pieces

1 cabbage, thinly sliced

1 cup of sliced spinach leaves

1 large yellow onion, sliced.

1 medium potato, diced

Boil all of the vegetables together until the potatoes are tender. Drain well.

Mix the vegetables into the pakora batter and fry at a temperature of 375 degrees, until golden brown, turning the pakora occasionally so that both sides brown evenly.

Single Vegetable Pakora

My favorite single vegetable pakora is potato, but you can really use any of your favorite vegetables or whatever you happen to have on hand.

Depending on the vegetable you use, you may need to cook the vegetable first. For example, potatoes should be sliced and boiled until barely tender, before making the pakora. Cauliflower should be cut into florets and boiled or steamed until just tender. Other vegetables such as onions and squash do not need to be cooked prior to being battered.

There are two ways to handle battering single vegetable pakora. For larger pieces of vegetables, such as potato or cauliflower, I like to dip the individual vegetables into the batter and drop each piece into hot oil. For onion pakora, I suggest cutting the onion into quarters, and then cutting the quartered onion into slices. Mix all of the onion slices into the pakora batter, and drop by the spoonful into the hot oil and cook until golden brown.

Regardless of whether or not you make single or mixed vegetable pakora, once the pakora has finished cooking, you'll want to drain it on paper towels and serve it with cilantro chutney or ketchup.

Cilantro Chutney

Cilantro chutney is an excellent way to add some variety to a meal. It goes great with Indian food such as pakoras, but can also be used as a healthy dressing for a salad, a topping for pasta, or a spread for a sandwich.

Ingredients

Serves 8

1 small coarsely chopped onion

1 coarsely chopped jalapeno

2 tsp sugar

1 1/2 tsp ground cumin

1 1/2 tsp salt

1/4 - 1/3 cup lime juice

1/4 cup olive oil

2 cups cilantro

3 cloves garlic

#1: Cut off and discard the stems from the cilantro.

#2: Coarsely chop the cilantro.

#3: Peel three cloves of garlic.

#4 Coarsely chop one onion.

#5: Cut a jalapeno into eight parts (more or less). Jalapenos get their heat from the veins and the seeds, so unless you like it really hot, remove most of the seeds and veins.

#6: Measure out your spices -- 2 teaspoons sugar, 1 1/2 teaspoons ground cumin and 1 1/2 teaspoons salt.

#7: Squeeze the juice from limes or use the lime juice you get in a bottle at the grocery store. You'll need 1/4 to 1/3 of a cup of lime juice.

#8: Place all of the above ingredients, along with the olive oil into a blender and blend until smooth.

Tip: If you don't like food too spicy, discard all or part of the jalapeno seeds

---

How to Make Authentic Indian Chai

As a person who has spent quite a bit of time in India as an ethnographer, I was delighted when I first saw that places in America such as Starbucks are serving chai. That is, until I ordered my first cup. Let me tell you, what we call, "chai" here in America and what they serve every day in India, are two different things!

In India, chai is a part of daily life, that goes beyond having something hot and delicious to drink. It is part of the culture and in many cases, the way a woman is perceived is at least somewhat dependent on her ability to make and serve chai properly.

Not only is it normal to make a pot of chai first thing in the morning, chai is also immediately prepared when people drop by for those ever present unannounced visits. Because of that, when living in India, one of the first things I had other women teach me how to do was how to make a proper pot of chai. This served me well as I was able to properly practice hospitality by serving chai and biscuits every time someone came for a visit.

First, one thing you should know about proper Indian chai is that it often contains no spices. As a cultural researcher who spent a year in India, I drank literally hundreds of cups of chai, and never once had chai that is spicy like it is when purchased here in the United States. When spices are used in chai in India, they are a very subtle addition to the chai that add just a hint of flavor. Chai in the United States is far spicier than chai in India. It isn't that it is wrong to put spices in chai if you like it that way, but just know that the ultra spicy chai we serve in America isn't what you'll typically find in India.

Because of that, I'm going to give you instructions for making chai without spices, and then let you know how to spice up the chai in a authentic Indian way if you are so inclined.

In an Indian kitchen, standard measuring tools are not used when making chai. Instead, you will use your tea cup to measure the water and milk. The instructions I'm providing are based on a smallish tea cup, not a mug. If you choose to use a mug, double the amount of loose tea leaves and sugar.

The beauty of using the tea cups to measure is that you can make precisely the number of cups of chai needed.

For EACH person you will serve chai to, do the following:

Place 1 teacup of water into a saucepan.

Add 1 heaping teaspoon of loose black tea leaves into the cold water. (Some Indians like to mix Lipton Red Label tea and Lipton Green Label tea. The mixture does provide a nice blend of flavor.)

Bring the water to a boil, and add in 1 teaspoon of sugar, and boil for 1 minute.

Add in one teacup of milk, and heat to boiling. Allow to boil for about 30 seconds, stirring so it doesn't boil over.

Strain and serve.

Notice that for one serving of chai I have 1 teacup of water, 1 heaping teaspoon of loose black tea, 1 teaspoon of sugar, and 1 teacup of milk. This provides more than one cup of chai per person! I do it this way for a couple of reasons. First of all, some of the water evaporates while boiling, Secondly, some people may want a second cup of chai. If I prepare chai in the way described above, I generally have just the right amount for all present, and everybody is happy.

Notice there are no spices in the above recipe. If you want to add spices to your chai, traditionally you will want to use a small piece of finely minced fresh ginger root in the winter or if making chai for someone with a cold, or a crushed cardamom pod or two in the summer. You may also use a powdered chai masala found in Indian grocery stores if you prefer a greater variety of spices, but add just a pinch for about four servings of chai. I like to add the spices in the cold water at the same time I add the tea leaves so the spices have time to infuse the water with flavor.

If making chai for company, I strain the chai as I pour it into a nice teapot and then serve my guests the chai directly from the teapot. If making chai for myself, I just use the strainer when pouring the chai directly from the pot into my tea cup.

I hope these instructions will help you to enjoy authentic Indian chai, no matter where in the world you live.

Pizza Hut -- The Best Pizza Ever!

When my family lived in India, we fell in love with the fusion pizzas served at Pizza Hut. In addition to standard favorites such as pepperoni that are served in the U.S. and most of the rest of the world, there was a variety of pizza options that had an Indian twist.

One such pizza, known as Chicken Tikka Pizza quickly became our favorite. After we returned to the U.S., we found ourselves craving Indian pizza. After a lot of trial and error, I finally came up with a recipe that at least closely resembles the pizza we ate in India.

Below is my own recipe for Chicken Tikka Pizza.

First, make the pizza dough. You may use the recipe below, use a favorite pizza dough recipe of your own, or start off with a store bought pizza crust. Please note that the recipe below is for two large pizzas.

Pizza Dough Recipe

4 cups lukewarm water

1.5 tbsp. yeast

1.5 tbsp. salt

6 cups flour

In a very large bowl combine the water, yeast and salt. Mix in the flour, using a dough whisk or your hands. It is not necessary to knead the dough. Allow the dough to rise for at least two hours.

While the dough is rising, prepare the Chicken Tikka.

Chicken Tikka

2 boneless chicken breasts, cut into 1-inch cubes

2 tbsp. plain yogurt

2 tsp. garlic ginger paste

2 tsp. lemon juice

1 tsp. crushed ajwain seeds

½ tsp. turmeric

1/8 tsp. cayenne pepper

½ tsp. garam masala

2 tbsp. oil

Salt to taste

Marinate chicken in all the ingredients except the butter for at least two hours. After the chicken has marinated, bake the chicken at 350 degrees for about 30 minutes, or until done.

Chicken Tikka Pizza Sauce

8-ounce can tomato sauce

2 tbsp. tikka masala or curry powder

2 tbsp. water

2 tbsp. oil

1/8 tsp. cayenne pepper

Combine all ingredients in a small bowl.

Chicken Tikka Toppings

Prepared chicken tikka

8 ounces mozzarella cheese

¼ thinly sliced red onion

1 bunch cilantro, stems removed and coarsely chopped

2 thinly sliced tomatoes

2 limes, cut into small wedges

Now it's time to assemble the pizza!

First, divide the dough into two portions. Roll each portion of dough out in a size and shape that fits the pizza pans you are using. I've used both large round pizza pans as well as large rectangular baking sheets for this recipe and both have worked fine. Just bear in mind that the smaller the pan, the thicker the crust will be, so choose extra large pans if you prefer a thinner crust.

Spread the pizza sauce evenly over the dough, then top with mozzarella cheese, chicken tikka, red onions, cilantro, sliced tomatoes and limes.

Remove the limes before eating, squeezing the juice from the limes on the pizza first if desired.

Yields: 2 large pizzas

McDonalds in India: Where's the Beef?

Westerners living in or visiting India enjoy a wonderful variety of food: dahl (a variety of spiced lentils), curried vegetables, wonderful breads baked in clay ovens, and McDonalds' fries and shakes.

Yes, that's right; McDonalds in India provides westerners with a little taste of home. Just don't expect the menu to be the same as it is in the U.S. Among other differences, you won't find beef on the menu.

Diets in India are often impacted by the many different religions in India. Hindus don't eat beef, so there is no beef on the McDonalds' menu in India. Muslims don't eat pork, so the McDonalds Corporation in India is quick to point out on their website (mcdonaldsinindia.com) that not only is there no beef, there is no pork or pork byproducts in any McDonalds restaurant in India.

Additionally, with the high number of vegetarians in India, about half of the menu at McDonalds in India is vegetarian, which makes it a good choice for diners who want some healthy options - whether or not they are vegetarian.

Here's a glimpse of what you can order at a McDonalds in India, along with a note about my favorite menu items that I personally consumed at McDonalds in India.

(Side note the menu items listed below are to give you an idea of what to expect at McDonalds in India, but all items may not still be on the menu, and there no doubt may be some new items as well at the time of your visit.)

Vegetarian Fare

McVeggie™

The McVeggie ™ sandwich starts with the oh-so-familiar sesame seed bun. In between the bread, you'll find a vegetarian patty that is made from peas, carrots, green beans, red bell pepper, potatoes, onions, rice, and seasoning. This vegetarian burger is garnished with lettuce, and has mayonnaise made without eggs spread thickly on the bread.

McAloo Tikki™

Potatoes (aloo in Hindi) are a popular filling food item in India. McDonald's in India's McAloo Tikki ™ sandwich includes a patty made out of potatoes, peas, and spices. It also includes tomato slices, onions, and vegetarian mayonnaise.

Paneer Salsa Wrap™

Paneer is referred to as cottage cheese in India, but it is nothing like what we call cottage cheese here in the U.S. It is made from milk but is similar in texture to tofu. McDonald's in India's Paneer

Salsa Wrap™ starts with a small slab of paneer that has been dredged in a coating that is a cross between Mexican and Cajun in flavor. I'm not sure if it is then fried or baked, but the coating is crunchy. The paneer patty is wrapped in flatbread and topped with a salad mixture that includes lettuce, red cabbage and celery and then is finished off with vegetarian mayonnaise, salsa and cheddar cheese.

Crispy Chinese

The Crispy Chinese sandwich is somewhat misnamed. It is crispy, but I'm not sure it resembles anything that I've ever eaten in a Chinese restaurant either in the U.S. or China. Nevertheless, this vegetarian patty which is topped with a creamy Schezwan sauce and lettuce is a nice addition to McDonald's in India's vegetarian menu.

Veg McCurry Pan™

I love the Veg McCurry Pan™!

If you are in the mood for something similar to pizza, but don't want a tomato-based sauce, McDonalds in India's Veg McCurry Pan™ is a good choice. It starts with a rectangular shaped crust that is topped with a creamy sauce (made without eggs), and vegetables including broccoli, baby corn, mushrooms and red bell pepper. It is then baked until the crust is crisp and the toppings are hot and bubbly.

Pizza McPuff™

The vegetarian Pizza McPuff™ is another favorite of mine. It also starts with a rectangular shaped crust, but instead of a creamy sauce is flavored with a tomato-based sauce and then is topped with carrots, beans, bell peppers, onions, peas and mozzarella cheese.

Non-Vegetarian Fare at McDonalds in India

Although I ate very little meat when I lived in India, on occasion I was in the mood to deviate from my regular vegetarian diet. When that urge struck, I knew that I could find something at McDonalds to satisfy my hunger. Here are the non-vegetarian food choices you might find at McDonalds in India:

Chicken Maharaja Mac™

At McDonalds in India, the Chicken Maharaja Mac ™ sandwich is made with 2 grilled chicken patties and is topped with onions, tomatoes, cheese and something similar to chipotle mayonnaise. [It's the Indian equivalent to the iconic Big Mac.]

McChicken™

If you're in the mood for chicken, but you want something less filling than the Chicken Maharaja Mac™, the McChicken™ sandwich is a good choice. It contains one breaded and fried chicken patty and is topped with lettuce and vegetarian mayonnaise. It is similar in size (but not taste) to the spicy chicken sandwich on the dollar menu at McDonalds restaurants in the U.S.

Filet-O-Fish™

The Filet-O-Fish™ sandwich at McDonalds in India is the only sandwich item on the menu that is exactly the same as the Filet-O-Fish sandwich you might eat at a McDonalds in the U.S. So if you really want a taste of home, the Filet-O-Fish™ sandwich is the sandwich to order.

Chicken Mexican Wrap™

The Chicken Mexican Wrap™ starts off with flatbread. Tucked inside the flatbread is a chicken patty that has been encrusted with a crunchy seasoning mixture that is a cross between Cajun and Mexican. It is the non-vegetarian counterpart to the Paneer Salsa Wrap. It's an excellent menu item, but if you are looking for something truly Mexican, you'll be disappointed with the Chicken Mexican Wrap™ because while I'm not sure what type of ethnic food it resembles, it's definitely not Mexican -- but still good.

Chicken McGrill™

The Chicken McGrill™ sandwich starts off with a grilled chicken patty that is embellished with cilantro mayonnaise, onions and tomatoes and is served on a toasted bun.

Chicken McCurry Pan™

The closest thing to Italian food at the McDonalds in India is the Chicken McCurry Pan™. It starts off with a rectangle of dough and is topped with a tomato-curry sauce, spiced with thyme, basil, and oregano. It is finished off with chicken, bell peppers, and cheese and is baked till crisp and bubbly. Delicious!

Familiar Fare at McDonalds in India

There are a couple of things that are exactly the same in a McDonalds in India as what you would consume at a McDonalds in the U.S. The identical menu items include the Filet-O-Fish (as mentioned above), McDonald's famous fries, shakes, and soft-served ice-cream, both sundaes and cones. They also serve

Chicken McNuggets, but currently only in the south. And of course soft drinks are available as well.

I don't eat at McDonalds in the U.S. very often, but when I lived in India, I ate there about once a week for many different reasons. First of all, when I was at McDonalds, I could pretend for the 30 minutes or hour I was there, that I was in the U.S. It wasn't that I didn't like India, but I did at times miss home, and McDonalds was one of the easiest ways for me as a foreigner to sooth my homesick tummy.

If your trip is a short one, you may not miss the food you're used to like I did on my longer trips, but there's another great reason to eat at McDonalds: When I went to McDonalds, I knew that I could find a clean restroom there that might even have toilet paper - a pretty rare thing in India. That detail made it a great place to stop for a meal or snack when I was out and about for a good amount of time on any given day.

The next time you're touring India, give McDonalds in India a try. You just might stumble across a menu item you wish was served in the U.S., you'll experience the blessed relief of air conditioning and have access to a clean bathroom. All things considered, dining at McDonalds in India will likely be a pleasant experience for you.

Sources: Personal experience and McDonalds in India website: www.mcdonaldsinindia.com

Other American Restaurant Chains in India

For the most part, I would encourage you to simply eat Indian food while in India, especially if you're there for only a week or two.

But if your trip is a longer one, and you want a taste of home, or if you just don't like Indian food, or (and this next reason is important!) you want air conditioning, cleanliness, and perhaps, just maybe, even toilet paper (please don't get your hopes up!), then in addition to heading to McDonalds or Pizza Hut, here are a couple of options for you:

- California Pizza Kitchen
- Hard Rock Café
- Krispy Kreme
- Quiznos
- Ruby Tuesday
- Subway
- Taco Bell
- TGIFridays

There are many others, as well, but of course not every city is going to have all of the restaurants, so if you really want to know what American restaurants are available where you'll be traveling, just do a quick Google search before you go, and make note of where in the city the various restaurants are so you'll be able to find them when you want.

One thing to keep in mind, however, is that the menus will be quite different than what you're used to, because they are made to accommodate Indian taste buds, often use ingredients that can be sourced from within India, and also accommodate religious dietary restrictions.

General Food Safety Guidelines

I once had a friend who went to India and packed enough trail mix to last her the entire time she was in the country. She did it so she wouldn't have to worry about what to eat or not eat. While I respect anyone's decision regarding what they'll do and not do when in India, it's kind of a pity that she missed out on all that great Indian food!

The good news is that it's relatively easy to stay healthy while in India, so long as you take the necessary precautions.

In addition to following the tips above for not getting sick when eating street food, keep these in mind as well:

- Avoid drinks with ice. Ice is, of course, made with water, and just because it's been frozen, doesn't mean that it won't get you sick. So skip the ice!
- A general rule of thumb with fruit and vegetables is to peel it, cook it, or forget it. For example, you don't really want to eat at a western-style salad bar that has fresh lettuce and other fresh veggies. (There aren't a ton of these in India anyway, but if you happen to see one, and it looks good, beware!)

On the other hand, eating something like sliced cucumbers that have been peeled is fine, and of course, cooked vegetables are fine as well.

- Water -- you should always drink bottled water when in India. Most likely water in a 5-star hotel will be properly filtered, but especially if you're in India for a short period of time, you don't want to have any of that time spoiled as a result of drinking unfiltered water.

Scams are an unfortunate part of India, and water is one area you need to be cautious. When you purchase bottled water, make sure to check to see if the seal has been broken. Some unscrupulous vendors refill water bottles with tap water, and sell them as if they are new. Needless to say, the last thing you want to do is drink Indian tap water!

TRUE STORY

When we lived in India the first time, our kitchen was equipped with an Aqua Guard water filter, and between that and purchasing bottled water, I didn't get sick during all the months I was there. For the most part, we just refilled our own water bottles using the filtered water in our kitchen.

Because of that, I was delighted to see an Aqua Guard filter in the kitchen in the flat we rented the next time we spent an extended amount of time in India. Unfortunately, during the six months we were there the second time, our entire family was sick, a lot.

I'll spare you most of the details, but to give you some indication of the outcome, sickness ranged from my husband being near out of his mind with hallucinations, and the rest of us just feeling like we wanted to die.

We were treated for parasites -- and trust me, the medication for that (at least the stuff we purchased at pharmacies in India) made us feel like our insides were being ripped out. Not fun, especially since we had to take it and then two weeks later take more to kill off any remaining parasites.

To make matters worse, not long after receiving treatment, we'd get sick again.

We finally discovered that the person who hooked up the water filter in our apartment hadn't actually hooked it up -- and so even though we were using the filter, we were drinking "pure" (if you can call it that), unfiltered Indian tap water.

Trust me -- you do not, I repeat, you do NOT want to do that!

A Smart Shopper's Guide to Shopping in India

I love some things about India, and am less than thrilled with some other aspects of it. One of the things I love is shopping, though I've had some maddening Indian shopping experiences as well. This section contains some tips for making your shopping experience in India one that you'll remember with fondness rather than regret.

Don't Be Afraid to Bargain When Shopping in India

Most westerners are unaccustomed to bargaining. We simply pay the listed price without much thought. But in India, especially as a foreigner, expect the initial asking price to be much higher than the true value of the item.

As a general rule of thumb, I often give a counter offer of about half of what the shop owner initially quoted as the price. For instance, if the shop owner says, "500 Rupees," I'll counter with, "250 Rupees." They may act shocked, but don't let that get to you! Just go on with the game, knowing that is how business is conducted there.

To test out whether or not the price you are offering is reasonable, if the shop owner rejects your offer, try walking away and see how the seller responds. They'll likely come after you and agree to the price you offered, or something close to it.

If they don't come after you, that means you offered a truly ridiculous price, and if you really want the item, you need to go back and offer more.

Look to See Who Else is Shopping

A sure way to know that you're shopping in a place that is overpriced is to look around at the other shoppers in the store. Are a lot of other foreigners shopping there? If everyone in the store is from the West, you're most likely in a place that has "special prices" for foreigners. Those prices are only special in the eyes of the merchants, but are a rip off for the shoppers. This is especially true if a rickshaw driver brought you to the store without you asking to go there; as mentioned in the scams section, they are paid a commission for everyone they bring to those shops. Instead, make your purchases in stores where Indians themselves shop.

Check the Quality of the Items

Although India has some amazing handicrafts and other items worth buying, the workmanship can sometimes be of a lower quality than what you're accustomed to. In order to avoid disappointment, be sure to check to see that everything is working properly. For instance, before buying a purse, make sure that the zippers work properly.

Shopping in India can be an amazing experience, and the items you'll bring home can bring you a great deal of pleasure in the years to come if you remember these few simple tips.

Here are some of the Amazing Things to Buy in India

Textiles: If you like fabric of any kind, and things made with fabric, India is going to be a shopper's paradise for you. You can find everything from cushion covers to wall hangings to ribbon and trims. Expect to see block printed fabric, fabric with mirrors, embroidery, etc. Truly wonderful!

Think a bit outside the box with this type of thing. For example, a sari is a single long piece of fabric, which can be used to all kinds of projects such as making window coverings.

Incense: If you like incense, chances are you can find a fragrance you love in India. Even if, like me, you don't burn incense for spiritual or religious reasons, it can still be a pleasant thing to bring home, as a reminder of your time in India.

Brass items: Brass items such as candle holders, and other decorative items made with brass are plentiful -- and very inexpensive.

Handmade paper goods, such as journals, notecards, etc.

"Blue" pottery. Jaipur is known for its "blue" pottery (which happens to be in colors other than just blue, which is why I put blue in quotes). You can get everything from beads to coasters to knobs along with all kinds of decorative items. You do have to be a bit careful, though, as these can be heavy and are definitely breakable. Neerja International

http://www.neerjainternational.com/ in Jaipur is the place I personally recommend, though there are many others as well.

Jewelry: You can get great deals on both costume jewelry as well as gold, silver and gemstones in India. You do have to be extremely careful when it comes to buying gemstones in India. The difficulty is that many gemstones are cut in India, particularly in Jaipur, which makes it a great place to shop for gemstones. Unfortunately, there are also many gemstone scams, so you really have to be cautious. The bottom line is that if it seems too good to be true. . .

Of course, you don't have the same worries with costume jewelry such as bangles. Just be sure to look them over to make sure there are no cracks, missing stones, etc.

Spices: Nowadays you can buy Indian spices in most any city, and certainly online if you don't have an Indian grocery store in your neighborhood. But you can find expensive spices such as saffron at a much better price in India.

Musical instruments: If you're musically inclined, or if you just want to use instruments as decoration, you can pick up some Indian instruments such as a tabla (small drum) and if you have the room for it and can get it home in one piece, a sitar is something most of your friends probably don't have!

Carved wood: I've bought everything from intricately carved wooden boxes to elephants. There are some cheaply done ones, for sure, but there are also many that are nicely done. The great thing about them is they are lightweight and durable enough that they aren't likely to be a problem to pack and carry back home.

Stone boxes with inlaid stones: One thing I love about these little boxes is that they are a great reminder of the Taj Mahal if that was one of your stops in India. Naturally, the inlaid stones in most boxes you see most likely aren't precious stones, but are still very beautiful.

Hindi pop music. Indian music -- especially the more traditional music -- can be hard on a westerner's ears, but Hindi pop music is a lot of fun and can definitely bring back pleasant memories of your trip.

Chess sets: You can find some beautiful chess sets that are made with stone such as marble. They make for a very classy gift, and something nice to display in your home.

In addition to the items listed above, simply keep your eyes peeled for anything that looks interesting. The main thing is to keep the tips provided earlier in mind when you shop, so you'll have a smile on your face, rather than regrets, once you get home with your treasures.

Family Life in India

The first time I went to India, I went with my two children, who were then 10 and 12 in tow. In my estimation, taking my kids to India was one of the best things I ever did for them, because it taught them a lot about the bigger world we live in, and helped them to be more adaptable.

Although I wouldn't hesitate to take children to India, there are a few things to keep in mind in order to make the trip enjoyable and safe. Read on for some of my best tips for traveling to India with children.

Prepare Your Children Ahead of Time for Food Safety Issues in India

As you've no doubt gathered by now, it's not uncommon for both adult and children foreign travelers to have "tummy troubles" when in India, and children may be less inclined to know what to avoid in order to at least reduce the chances of picking up parasites and other undesirable causes of illness.

Now chances are, if you're only in India for a short period of time, you may be able to supervise your children 100% of the time and make sure they don't eat or drink anything they shouldn't. But kids can, at times, do something in the blink of an eye, before you have a chance to stop them. Because of this, it's helpful to talk with your kids ahead of time to let them know the basics of what to watch out for.

If you're traveling with children under the age of 10, rather than give them a long list of what they can and cannot eat and expecting them to keep it straight, instruct your children not to eat or drink anything without your permission. Children in India are typically expected to follow the lead of their parents, so it will not seem strange or rude for your children to ask permission before eating or drinking anything there.

Older children can be instructed to avoid the following:

- •Water not in a sealed bottle
- •Unpeeled fruit or vegetables
- •Food prepared in dirty kitchens (including food from many street vendors)

Prepare Your Children for Traffic Safety Issues in India

One of the hardest things for me to adapt to in India was the traffic, and the seeming absence of traffic rules. After I'd been there for a while, I began to see that there was some logic behind the traffic habits and patterns, but it was somewhat hard for me as a westerner to grasp.

Let your kids know that crossing the street in India can be very different than the U.S. or other Western countries and that even if they do not have to do so in the U.S., you may need to hold their hands when crossing the street in India.

It's true that they may balk about this, but use your best judgment on it. You know your children best, and whether they will follow your instruction or do whatever they want in spite of what you say. If they fit into the "do whatever they want" or perhaps simply tend to forget what you've told them, or absentmindedly do things, then hand holding may be in order. Again, use your best judgment. Just know that you have to be stricter about this in India than you do in your home country.

Help Your Children Understand Cultural Differences in India

Foreigners are given a certain amount of grace in India, and aren't expected to do everything right. This is even more true with children. Even so, letting your kids know ahead of time how to be respectful in India is a great way to teach them to be sensitive to others and will also help endear your entire family to the people of India.

One area of difference is food. Teach your children not to eat food using their left hand, and to avoid passing food to others using their left hands.

Let your children know ahead of time that due to religious restrictions, beef and pork are not consumed in many parts of India, and that even McDonalds will not have hamburgers!

Prepare them to behave appropriately before visiting any religious buildings such as mosques and temples.

Have them wear shoes they can easily remove before entering buildings or even rooms that are considered holy by Indian people. This is where it's important for you as a parent to pay attention to what others around you are doing so you will know how to properly instruct your children about how to behave in sacred places unfamiliar to you.

Prepare Your Children for Poverty in India

Poverty can -- and should -- be disturbing, but I believe being exposed to poverty in India was one of the best things for my children. Besides that, poverty cannot be avoided, and since your children will be sure to see it, it is best to prepare them ahead of time. This can be done by simply talking about it, and viewing some photos that show some India street and slum scenes.

Tips for Couples

Public display of affection (PDA) may be normal in the West, but it is not normal in India. Even things as innocent as holding hands, should be avoided, even by married couples, when in public. So save any affection for when you're in the privacy of your hotel room.

Obviously, it is fine to touch for safety reasons -- such as a husband offering his hand to his wife when she's climbing down from a train or other place where she may feel a bit unsteady.

Needless to say, if hand holding can be seen as inappropriate, kissing in public is a definite no-no, so just don't do it.

Yes, you may "get away with it," but why be unnecessarily offensive?

Homosexuality

You may see two men holding hands in India. That doesn't mean they're gay; that type of affection between men is normal there, and is just an indication of friendship.

It's important to note that homosexuality is still very much a taboo subject in India that is seldom discussed, and not only is it taboo, it's illegal.

Would tourists who are openly gay be prosecuted? That would be HIGHLY unlikely, but the bottom line is that whether you agree with it or not, my advice is to respect the culture, and avoid doing anything that would be unnecessarily offensive.

Remember that ideas about sexuality and affection, even among heterosexual married couples is different in India than it is in the West, so regardless of whether you're gay or straight, your sexuality needs to be kept private when in India.

Religion

A Guide to Religious Etiquette in India

India is a land of cultural and religious diversity. Unlike the Western world, religion permeates every facet of life in India. I recall that on my first trip to India, I was surprised to see religious icons everywhere I went, including places of business such as banks and grocery stores. Since religion is such a big part of life in India, it is important for visitors -- including those who are not themselves particularly religious -- to prepare themselves for the proper way to show respect in religious settings in India.

The good news is, although the religions are very diverse in India, many of the same rules of etiquette apply, regardless of the religion, because when it comes right down to it, many of the rules are based on showing respect.

Here are the two main things to keep in mind, when you visit a church, mosque, or temple in India.

Remove Your Shoes Before Entering Religious Buildings in India

There is some variation from one building to another when it comes to the need to remove shoes before entering a place of worship in India. For instance, every time I visited a Hindu temple, or even stepped into a puja room (shrine) in a private home, I was expected to remove my shoes. In contrast, some, but not all Christian churches required me to take off my shoes.

The good news is, it doesn't take long to figure out whether or not to remove your shoes, as you can simply look to see what everyone else around you does.

Some places of worship have a place where you can "check in" your shoes and get a token of some sort that is used to claim the shoes when you come out of the temple. In others, people simple leave their shoes outside the entrance of the place of worship.

HOT TIP

Be forewarned that the pavement surrounding the place of worship may be hot. On many occasions I wished I had a pair of socks with me to protect the soles of my feet, so you might want to have a pair along with you, just in case.

Women Should Cover Their Heads in Places of Worship in India

When a woman covers her head in India, it is a sign of respect. For example, if a women is in the presence of dignitaries, or depending on the family, in the presence of her father-in-law or perhaps even her husband, a woman should cover her head as a way of showing respect.

Therefore, when entering a place of worship in India, women should make a point of covering their heads. In Christian churches, women may not always cover their heads when entering the church, but will be expected to cover their heads during prayer.

Indian clothing for women, such as saris and the popular salwar kameez are made in such a way that the pallu (fabric that goes over the shoulder of a sari), and the dupatta (scarf worn across the chest when wearing a salwar kameez), are used to cover the head when needed.

HOT TIP

If wearing western clothing, a woman can carry a scarf with her to use to cover her head when in places of worship in India.

Let's take a look at the most common religions in India. I'll provide basic information on each of the religions, presenting them in the following order, based on the percentage of people in India who practice the specific religion:

- Hinduism: 80.5%
- Islam: 13.4%
- Christianity: 2.3%
- Sikhism: 1.9%
- Buddhism: 0.8%
- Jainism: 0.4%

In case you noticed, that doesn't quite add up to 100%. The remaining 0.7% is made up of "other" religions which I won't address.

Also, one thing to note is that different regions may have a dominate religion, where the percentages listed above are inaccurate for that region. For instance, using Christianity as an example, the northeastern state of Nagaland has an extremely high percentage of Christians (90%) and south Indian states such as Kerala tend to have a higher population of Christians (19.2%) compared to the rest of the country.

In contrast, the northwestern state of Gujarat is 0.43% Christian, and the state where I spent most of my time in India (Rajasthan) isn't even listed as a state with a significant Christian population. Indeed, during the time that I spent in the Rajasthan city of Jodhpur, I didn't see any churches to attend, and for that matter, didn't meet any Christians while there.

(See this Wikipedia article for more statistics on religion in India: http://en.wikipedia.org/wiki/Christianity_in_India.)

One thing you'll note is that I go into more depth about Christianity than I do about the other religions, since that is my own religion. While I never had a church to attend in Jodhpur, when I lived in Jaipur, even though it is also in Rajasthan, with it being a larger city, there were a few churches there that I attended. I'll share some of my church experiences, along with some experiences I had at a Christian conference in Central India.

I'll also share some personal experiences with Hinduism, since the majority of my friends in India are Hindus, but I write about those as an outsider, no doubt about it.

Without further ado, let's go ahead and dive in to the fascinating world of religion in India!

Hinduism

Hinduism is hard to define, because it's more of a way of life than a religion, though no doubt about it, there are strong religious components to it.

I have to tell you that even though I spent time as a cultural researcher and with a focus on a specific caste that are Hindus, I have to admit that I still don't really "get" Hinduism. Since the

Hindu way of thinking is so different from the western mindset, it was a bit hard to wrap my mind around it.

Here are a few main components of Hinduism to be aware of:

Millions of gods. Whereas some religions focus on a single God, Hinduism has a pantheon of gods. The exact number of gods is unknown, and any Hindu I've asked gave me a different answer to that question! In spite of there being millions of gods, there is a hierarchy of sorts, with Brahma being at the top, and there also being a trinity that consists of Vishnu, Shiva and Shakti -- and the other gods flowing from those three.

Now I can already tell you that there will be some Hindus who won't agree with what I just wrote. I've heard it said that in India, when something is true, the opposite is also true, so I won't even pretend to present something on Hinduism in an authoritative way, since it seems even many Indians themselves struggle with that.

As a non-Hindu, how can I possible get it right? The point is there are millions of gods, and each Hindu often is devoted to more than one god.

Astrology: This was one of the surprising things to me that I discovered upon my first visit to India.

Astrology can be seen as more powerful than the gods themselves. One of my Hindu friends told me that the gods are like an umbrella. In the same way that an umbrella doesn't stop the rain, but only shields you from the impact of the rain, the gods can't stop what the stars determine -- they can only help to reduce the impact. This same friend stated, "if the stars are against you, even the gods can't help."

Astrology impacts every area of a Hindu's life, such as marriage. I'll cover some of the marriage traditions in the culture section of this book, so for now will just say that prior to getting married, the prospective bride and groom have a pundit (Hindu priest) check their horoscopes, to make sure they match properly. If not, no marriage for them.

The stars also indicate times that are most auspicious for events, such as weddings to take place. This is why, based on the lunar calendar, numerous weddings occur in a very short period of time.

The bottom line is that astrology is very, very important to Hindus.

Reincarnation: Reincarnation is the process of birth, life and rebirth that happens multiple times. It is believed to continue until someone reaches nirvana.

Another strong component of this belief is that the life you are born into today is based on the life you lived previously, and that what you do in this life will impact the next life you life.

As an example, someone who is lower caste may be deemed to have lived a not-so-great life in the past, and thus they were, in a sense, "punished" by coming back as a lower caste person (if you're confused by the issue of caste, I'll explain that a bit more in the culture section). In contrast, a person born into a higher caste may believe that they were exceptionally good in a previous life, and were therefore rewarded in this life.

It should also be noted that people can be reincarnated as something lower than human.

Hindu Temples: Hindu worship is different from many other religions in that there aren't "services" to attend. So you won't see signs posted on temples that have times when various events take place. It's more of a "drop in when you can" type of approach to religion.

Having said that, morning seems to be a busy time, especially for the devout, who often start their day with a visit to the temple.

Islam

The word, "Islam" comes from an Arabic word that means peace, or submission, and the underlying message here is that the only way to have peace is to submit to God. Unlike Hindus, Muslims believe that there is only one God, the creator God, whom they refer to as Allah.

A quick word on getting the terms straight, between Islam and Muslim. Islam is the religion, and Muslims are the people who practice the religion. Therefore, it's improper to refer to the religion as Muslim, or to the people as Islams.

- As is true with many religions, in Islam, the religion is made up of a combination of both faith and works. Not only do Muslims "believe," they also, "do." The "doing" is focused on the following five pillars:
- Testimony of faith
- Prayer: Prayer happens five times a day, based on sun and geography. For instance, the first prayer of the day is Fajr, which occurs at dawn, and Maghrib occurs when the sun sets.
- Almsgiving: As is true with most religions, giving to the poor is a major component of Islam.
- Fasting: The most common time of fasting is Ramadan, which is the 9th month in the Islamic calendar. It is a month-long fast that takes place between sunrise and sunset. After sunset, community meals are common.

- Pilgrimage: Referred to as "Hajj," this pilgrimage is required to be done once in a lifetime by Muslims who are both physically and financially capable of making the journey to Mecca, which is located in Saudi Arabia

In terms of what you will experience in India when it comes to Islam will likely be hearing the call to prayer five times a day if you happen to be nearby a Mosque. The call to prayer goes out from the Mosque over a loudspeaker. Our family was often awakened early in the morning by the first call to prayer that takes place just as the sun is rising.

Christianity

Christianity in India refers to Christians of all stripes, be that Catholic or Protestant, or even what is likely deemed by many (Indian and non-Indian alike) as cults. Basically any faith that follows Christ in some way is counted as Christian in the numbers.

As a Christian myself, one of the things that struck me the most is that Christianity in India is passed down through the generations, and while that may be true in the West, it's more true in India. For example, a person is considered a Christian even if he doesn't believe in God, if his grandparents, parents, and so on are Christian.

One Indian friend of mine emphasized this to me without even realizing he was doing so when he said that he wanted to marry someone who is not just a Christian, but a "believer."

Attending Church in India

If you happen to have an opportunity to visit a church in India, keep in mind some of the religious etiquette tips presented above.

Also, most likely any church you attend will have men on one side of the church and women on the other. It will be obvious which side of the church you should sit on, as soon as you walk in. Children generally sit on the "women's" side of the church, regardless of gender.

Depending on location, church services may be in both English and the dominant Indian language of the region. For example, at the church I attended in Jaipur, the sermon was generally presented in Hindi and interpreted in English.

One thing to note, however, is that because of sometimes heavy accents, just because there is English interpretation doesn't mean you'll understand what's said! I'll never forget the time my daughter, who was 16 at the time asked me, "Mom, which one is speaking English and which one is speaking Hindi?" In addition to the heavy accents, I noticed that sometimes the speakers would switch whether they were speaking Hindi or English, which did a number on my brain, as I tried to follow what was said! Having said that, the interpretation is still helpful compared to the service being 100% Hindi.

Both Communion and Baptism are Serious

From what I've seen, Indian Christians aren't baptized as children, as they often are in the U.S. This is because baptism is a clear breaking away from any other gods that are often worshipped in India. With Hinduism having a pantheon of gods, it is okay for a Hindu to worship Jesus along side other gods.

But baptism is a public declaration that Jesus is THE God the person worships. This is a serious declaration that, depending on the location of the person could result in trouble, such as potential job loss, being rejected by family, and so on. (This is not true all places in India, but primarily in places and castes where Christianity is less accepted.)

TRUE STORY

I had always known baptism was serious, but it wasn't until our family was about to partake of communion at a church in Jaipur that I realized how serious it was. Our son, who was going on 14 at the time was practically tackled when he reached for the communion elements.

While this was rather shocking, once we understood their motives, we appreciated their "concern." The deal was that (at least at this particular church), unless you had been baptized, you couldn't take communion. Communion was for those who were "all in" which was demonstrated by baptism. My son was not only younger than most who have been baptized in India, he was also very small for his age, so the assumption was that there was no way he had been baptized, and therefore should not take communion.

Once it was made clear he had been baptized, he was able to take communion.

While I'm a Christian myself, most of my experience in India was pretty far removed from Christianity. I really didn't realize how far removed it was until I went to India to speak at a Christian women's conference.

Here's what that experience was like, along with some of the lessons I learned through the experience.

TRUE STORY

The director of the mission in India greeted me in my hotel lobby with a bouquet of flowers. That was a nice gesture, and I accepted them gladly. What I didn't know was that the tasteful bouquet of flowers was only a small token of appreciation compared to what awaited me.

We got into a hired jeep and drove five hours to the Girl's Christian Institute. We pulled up to a large iron gate and got out of the jeep. The gate kept me from seeing what was inside, and I was unprepared.

I'm not sure if it was jet lag, sheer exhaustion or what, but I somehow didn't immediately notice that the path I was about to walk on was lined with girls, so I was totally caught off guard when cheers broke out, and even more surprised when all the little girls start throwing flowers at me.

After the flower pelting ceremony, I was invited in for lunch, where a large feast awaited me. It was clear they had gone to a lot of trouble for me, and clearly tried to prepare food that a westerner would enjoy, including such favorites as "smashed potatoes."

As if the flower pelting ceremony and lunch were not enough, I was then brought into another room where all the girls came in and put on a program for me. Among other things, they sang and danced for me.

I can't even tell you what all happened on that same day, but in the photo above you can see that I'm wearing multiple garlands and have my hands full, of at least one other bouquet of flowers.

It's not always easy to receive, but particularly if you are a foreign guest at an event of some sort, be prepared to have gifts poured out on you. You may not expect or want them, but it's important to receive them graciously as a way of blessing the givers of the gifts.

Go with the Flow

There may be a lot that happens that you don't understand. That was certain the case for me. The good news is, you don't have to understand what's happening to participate; just give it your best shot!

For example, in the photo above, I have no idea why she was lighting a candle with one hand and had her other hand on a Bible. I noticed that the ribbon that was on the candle had caught on fire, which is probably why I look a little tentative, but no one else seemed to be bothered by it so I decided not to worry about it.

Accept the Fact That You're Going to Look Stupid Sometimes

"The women would like you to release the souvenir," the director of the organization told me.

"Sure, I'd be happy to," I replied.

I immediately began flipping through the file folders in my mind, trying to recall what it means to release a souvenir. Apparently that file in my brain was empty, because I had no idea what the souvenir would be and how I would "release" it. (Was I supposed to throw it or what?)

"When I release the souvenir, what do I need to do?" I asked.

"You just say, 'I release the souvenir.'"

That certainly sounded easy enough, but I had a niggling feeling in the back of my mind that there had to be more to it than that, so right before the souvenir releasing ceremony, I again asked the director, "So what do I need to do?" Again he replied, "You say, 'I release the souvenir.'"

Well, alrighty. I should be able to handle that.

Then again, maybe not.

After I got up on the platform, I was handed a beautifully packaged something -- apparently the souvenir. I assumed I was supposed to unwrap it, so began doing so. That seemed to be the right thing to do, as no one gasped or stopped me.

The trouble came when I spoke the words, "I release the souvenir." Close your eyes and imagine for a moment, what may have happened when I spoke those words. Are you ready to find out? If so, open your eyes.

What happened?

NOTHING. Nothing happened. It was dead silent. That was the first and only time I've experienced absolute silence in India. Something was obviously wrong.

I cleared my throat and again said (a little louder this time), "I release the souvenir!"

Again, nothing.

Thankfully, the director was standing next to me, so I leaned over toward him and whispered, "What am I supposed to do?"

He replied, "You say, 'I release the souvenir IN THE NAME OF THE LORD.'"

I approached the mic, and boldly proclaimed, "I release the souvenir in the name of the Lord" and the crowd went wild. (The photo at the top of this section is of me immediately after releasing the souvenir. I was feeling great relief at that moment!)

I suppose everyone knows that when you release a souvenir you are supposed to say, "In the name of the Lord." Silly me!

Be Prepared to Stand Out in the Crowd

India is the only place I'm taller than everyone.

There were times I longed to be invisible. It's not always easy, especially for introverts to receive a lot of attention everywhere they go, but it's a fact of life, particularly if you go to a country with few foreigners, and especially if your skin color is different from everyone else's.

Remember That You're Not the Only One Who Is Uncomfortable

It wasn't until after I received this photo that I saw that the teacher was pushing the children forward to shake hands with me. Now obviously, kids are often shy, but they are not the only ones who may feel uncomfortable with "the strange white lady" (or whatever you are).

In the same way that you may feel uncomfortable and be unsure of exactly what to do in particular situations, the nationals you're interacting with may also feel intimidated by your presence. Sure, they have the advantage of being on their own turf, but particularly if they are not used to interacting with foreigners, they may be uncomfortable.

Do your best to understand and then follow the culture where you are. In India that meant, among other things, eating with my hands, wearing Indian clothing, and covering my head during prayer. Don't be afraid to ask questions about what is appropriate, and pay attention to what other people around you are doing.

Buddhism

I often think of Buddhism as being a Thai or Japanese religion, but it actually originated in India in the 6th century in the state that is now known as Bihar. It declined significantly in India around the 13th century.

It is still practiced in India, mostly in the Himalayan region.

One of the most significant times of growth in Buddhism in India came about as a result of what is known as the Dalit-Buddhist movement, which you can read about here: http://en.wikipedia.org/wiki/Dalit_Buddhist_movement.

The basic idea behind this movement is that Dalits (low-cast Hindus, considered "untouchable") will have much more freedom and respect if they leave Hinduism and covert to Buddhism. I'm not sure how successful that movement has been, but it certainly makes sense from the perspective that those who are the lowest of the low (as far as caste is concerned), having nothing to lose by converting to another religion.

Jainism

Jainism has been around for a long time, and in fact has existed side by side next to Hinduism, pretty much from the beginning. The name, "Jainism" comes from the Sanskrit word which means, "follower of Jina or conqueror."

Even though Jainism is a minority religion, you may encounter it in an unusual place in India -- restaurants. In fact, some menus in India indicate that certain menu items are "Jain specials" or use some other type of terminology to indicate the particular dish is safe for Jains to eat.

Dietary restrictions based on religion are nothing unusual in India, but Jains take the restrictions further than most. Not only are they vegetarian, they also refuse to eat certain vegetables such as root vegetables, or anything that grows under the ground. For example, garlic, onions, and ginger are very common in Indian cooking, but Jains won't eat them since they grow beneath the surface of the soil.

The reason for this is because Jains practice what is called, "ahimsa" which is the focus of non-injury to all living things. The problem with vegetables that grow beneath the ground is that it's possible that while they are being harvested, insects will be killed. (I've often wondered about this one, because no doubt insets are killed when plants that grow above the ground are harvested, but I suppose that cannot be avoided altogether, and Jains, of course, have to eat something!)

Jains do other things to avoid inadvertently killing insects. The most devout Jains may wear muslin cloths over their mouths to keep them from inadvertently swallowing a small, flying insect.

Some even use small brooms to gently brush aside any small insects they may not even see, so they can avoid stepping on them.

The teachers of the religion, known as "Tirthankaras," teach that the way to be awakened is to renounce the world, and live a life of austerity.

There are two main traditions of Jainism -- the Shvetambaras ("white clad" monastics) and Digambaras ("sky clad" monastics). As the names imply, the different traditions indicate what type of clothing can be worn. Shvetambaras believe it's permissible to wear white robes, and those who practice Digambaras believe you should only be clad with the "sky" -- which means being naked.

Not all Jains follow such strict dress (or undress) codes. The strictness is more for Jains who are monks. No doubt Jains were present in the cities where we lived (or at least in Jaipur, since I saw "Jain Specials" on menus there), but I don't recall ever seeing anyone in a white robe. I did, on occasion see some people in India who were totally naked, but since that was a bit outside of my comfort zone, I never got up close and personal enough to ask them why they were naked, though generally speaking, the naked ones are likely some type of holy men.

Naked or not, Jains are focused on attaining nirvana, and depending on which Jain tradition one follows, this may be considered impossible for women. Shvetambaras believe that women can achieve nirvana, but Digambaras believe that the only way a woman can achieve nirvana is if she is first reincarnated as a man.

Culture

In addition to there being an abundance of people, one thing India has a lot of, is culture. Entire books can be written on this subject and still not dive deeply enough into it, so this section barely scratches the surface of all that Indian culture has to offer.

Naturally, some of Indian culture is good, and some is bad, as is true with all cultures.

Regardless of the bad, the culture is one aspect of India that you can't miss, and I'd encourage you to dive as deeply into it as you can.

As an outsider, you'll never be able to experience it fully, but if nothing else, use the information in this section to help you understand some of what you'll see and experience.

The Caste System

The caste system is one of the hardest things to accept about India, and one of the things that flies in the face of what those of us in the Western world tend to believe about equality.

It's a complex system that I can't go into in depth in this book, but the short version is that caste is a ranking system of sorts, that categorizes people based on the caste they are born into.

This is one of the hardest aspects for me to deal with, because people can't help the family they are born into.

Here are the four primary classes of people in India:

- **Brahmins** are the Hindu priests. Naturally, not every Brahmin is a priest, but all Hindu priests are Brahmins. They are traditionally trained in the Vedic scriptures, and in knowing how to perform various religious sacraments and ceremonies. Brahmins are the highest class in the caste system.

- **Kshatriyas** are the second highest class, and are administrators and warriors. A lot of Kshatriyas are in government and military positions, though some also run businesses. The Rajas this book was partly titled after are Indian royalty and are part of the Kshatriya class.

- **Vaishyas** are the third highest class, and were traditionally land cultivators and traders.

- **Shudras** is the fourth and lowest class, and the class that makes those of us in the West the most uncomfortable. These are typically servants, and many of them do menial tasks such as street sweeping (done with a broom). They are often treated as subhuman and have been called by many "untouchables."

Discrimination based on caste is illegal, and yet it still happens and is very common. Before you feel too indignant, it's important to admit that in the West, we too, discriminate at times, even though it's illegal. For instance, an older person may have a harder time getting a job, even though age discrimination is illegal.

The biggest difference that I see when it comes to a discriminatory mindset in India vs. the U.S. is that it's more widespread in India, has deeper roots, and is harder for people to break free from.

Speculation on my part regarding this is that it is due in part to the belief in reincarnation, and what you experience in this life being based to some degree on what you deserve, as a result of what you've done in the past. I recall one of my high-caste friends making the statement, "I must have been really good in my past life to get all this," in reference to the abundance of good fortune, including wealth.

This mindset can cause people to, at least on a subconscious level, feel justified in their discrimination, as people may be seen as "getting what they deserve."

A second thing that I think contributes to the discrimination is that it's hard to hide your background. This is true in the Western world when it comes to things like race -- if people see you, it may be obvious that you are of a certain ethnicity, for example. But in India it goes even deeper than that because a person's name is tied to their caste. So if you know someone's surname, you automatically have information regarding things such as their caste.

The good news is that things are changing when it comes to discrimination, but the bad news is that the changes are slow to come, and there's still a very long way to go when it comes to discrimination based on caste being a thing of the past in India.

From my perspective, the best thing you can do regarding caste is to treat all people with respect, regardless of how "lowly" they may be. For instance, the bicycle rickshaw driver may be wearing stained and worn out clothing, but treat him with kindness -- and give him a good tip -- any way.

As a foreigner, especially one who is just visiting, there isn't a whole lot you can do about discrimination based on caste. But you can certainly make someone's day a bit brighter by treating them with kindness.

An Indian Manners Guide for Foreign Travelers to India

To make the most of your trip to India, you may want to stay in guest houses, rather than fancy American hotel chains. That's an excellent choice for travelers who want to experience India as it really is because you will rent a room from an Indian family that will likely serve not only as your host, but also as your tour guide. However, it also means you will be more likely to mix with Indian nationals who may be offended by your American ways. The tips in this chapter will keep you from inadvertently offending your gracious Indian hosts.

Indian Meal Etiquette

Meals are a great time to connect with your host family in India. It is also a great time to offend people, if you're not careful. Keep the following in mind during meals in India and you'll be sure to please your hosts:

- Never use your left hand for eating or for passing food to other people.

- Even if silverware is provided for you, eat with your fingers, rather than forks and spoons.

- Clean your plate. Even if you don't like the taste of something, if you put it on your plate, you need to eat it, so start with small portions and then after eating all on your plate, take more of foods you like.

Clothing Standards in India

India defines modesty differently than those in the Western world. Women travelers should not wear the following:

- Shorts, including capris
- Sleeveless tops
- Tight pants

Instead, if possible, wear Indian clothing such as loose fitting and comfortable salwar kameezes that you can pick up anywhere in India, or online on sites such as eBay. If you prefer not to wear Indian clothing, wear long, loose fitting skirts with loose blouses with sleeves.

Clothing standards for men in India are more similar to American clothing norms, but shorts and jeans should be avoided. Business casual is a good bet for men traveling in India.

When No Means Yes in India

Your host may offer you tea. You may decline. A few minutes later they may offer it again, and you decline again. The third time they offer you tea, you may finally give in to the pressure and accept tea, even if you don't want it. That happened to me numerous times when I first lived in India and didn't know the rule that no doesn't mean no until you've said it three times. To avoid doing things or eating and drinking things you don't want, be prepared to say no three times before the matter will be dropped.

Feet Can Be Offensive in India

At the end of a long day of touring you may be tempted to sit down on the floor, with your legs stretched out. If you do so, be sure not to point the bottom of your feet toward another person, particularly an Indian person. Such a posture may be perfectly acceptable in the U.S. but is very offensive in India.

Arranged Marriages

One of the vast ways that India is different from the western world is in the custom of arranged marriages.

Prior to going to India as a cultural researcher, I had a pretty major misunderstanding of the topic of arranged marriages and in fact had a fairly negative attitude regarding arranged marriages.

However, one of the most important aspects of cultural research is putting aside your own beliefs, opinions, and preconceived ideas in order to see more clearly. Thus, I had to put aside my negative opinions about arranged marriages in order to explore the subject with integrity.

What I found surprised me. I found that arranged marriages aren't necessarily a bad thing!

Typically, the burden for the arrangement of the marriage is on the parents. It is the father's responsibility to choose and make the arrangements for a husband for his daughter. This presents a great deal of pressure for the father, and a great deal of shame if he has not arranged a marriage for his daughter by a particular age. (The optimal age depends on various factors such as caste, education level, etc.)

It might seem like an easy matter for a father to arrange the marriage, but a lot of factors must be considered. For instance, generally speaking, marrying outside of one's own caste is frowned upon, so that limits the number of choices.

Also, since the majority of Indians are Hindu, and Hindus believe strongly in astrology, the perspective couple's horoscopes must be analyzed and "suitably matched" or the marriage cannot take place. Additionally, the father will want to make sure that his daughter is marrying into a good family, so a lot of investigation needs to happen before the arrangements are made. The entire issue of arranging a marriage is one of the biggest responsibilities Indian parents face.

Now no doubt there are many unhappy people in arranged marriages, but to be fair, there are also many unhappy people in what Indian's call, "love marriages" -- the typical way we get married in the West.

One thing to keep in mind is that while there may be some rotten things about arranged marriages, whether in the East or West, parents want what is best for their children, and with few exceptions, do their best to make suitable marriage arrangements for their children.

One young single Indian woman said to me, "Of course my parents will choose a good husband for me. They love me. Why would they do anything less than choose a good husband for me?" She had confidence that her parents not only loved her and had her best interest at heart, but that they also had more wisdom than she did and could make a better decision for her in the area of marriage.

Most Indians frown on "love marriages." Love marriages do take place in India, but often without the support of friends or family. And in fact, many people in India feel that love marriages are doomed to failure. Their attitude is not based purely on prejudice regarding love marriages, but in fact is based on a higher divorce rate of those whose marriages were not arranged by the parents.

Although most westerners cannot fathom marrying someone they do not love, it does have its practical points. Most Indians are quick to point out that the divorce rate in India is only 2%, compared to parts of the world where 50% or more of the love marriages end in divorce.

This can be attributed to the fact that marriage in India is not based on feelings, but rather on commitment.

One Indian woman said to me, "Here, we get married without having feelings for the person. We base our marriage on commitment, not on feelings. As our marriage progresses, the feelings develop. In America, you base your decision to marry on feelings, but what happens when the feelings wane? You have nothing left to keep the marriage together if you get married according to feelings and then the feelings go away." I had to admit that she had a good point!

Although it would be hard for me to fathom arranged marriages in the U.S., as I researched arranged marriages in India, I experienced a higher degree of appreciation for this aspect of Indian culture.

Finding a Spouse

Since Indians typically do not date, and do not have "love marriages," how then do people in India find a spouse?

Finding a spouse in India can be rather complicated. For one thing, there are greater restrictions regarding who one can marry. For instance, although inter-caste marriage does happen, and is perhaps becoming more common, it is still largely frowned on.

Also, as mentioned, astrology plays a big part in who a person can marry. That issue doesn't come into play, however, until a potential spouse has been located. At that time, both the potential bride and groom will hand their horoscopes over to a Hindu priest known as a pundit. The pundit will analyze the horoscope signs called janat patri to see which ones complement each other and which ones cancel each other out.

A significant number of the janat patri must match, or the marriage cannot take place. If the horoscopes don't match, the process of finding a spouse starts all over again.

Since the process of finding a spouse in India can be rather complicated, many means are used to assist the Indian parents of the potential bride or groom as they search for a suitable spouse for their son or daughter. Here are some of those means.

The local barber can help a person in India find a spouse.

A barber may seem like an unlikely matchmaker, but they play a significant role for the following reasons. First, the family will typically have the same barber (or relatives of the same barber) for generations. The barber also has connections with many other families, and knows much of the gossip of the various families.

The potential bride's family may ask the barber for help in scoping out the potential groom's family. The barber may be able to help determine the family's financial status, and what type of character, business sense, and so on, the potential groom has. As strange as this may sound, our team of ethnographers heard about the important role a barber can play from many of our cultural helpers!

Family and friends can help a person in India find a spouse.

Networking is a big deal in the West, but we certainly have nothing over the people in India when it comes to networking. Everyone in India knows someone who knows someone who knows someone.

I once attended a large Hindu festival with some Indian friends. They demonstrated to me how this works, by going up to total strangers and talking to them. Generally, in the first 30 seconds of the conversation, they would discover some connection, which would help them size up the other person. They would have some common (but distant) relatives, family members who attend the same school, and so on. These connections are important because it helps them to follow up with a more thorough investigation about the person. For instance, if both families have relatives attending the same school, it is relatively easy to learn the reputation of the potential bride or groom.

Also, if an Indian person asks their relatives for recommendations for a spouse for one of their children, the relative they ask may well know someone who might be suitable. Since marriage is such a big deal in India, it is not unusual or uncommon to ask such questions nor is it uncommon for people to always be on the lookout for potential spouses for their friends or relatives.

Newspaper classified ads may help a person in India find a spouse.

It is not uncommon for a newspaper to have a large section of classified ads for those looking to marry. This is quite different from the personal ads here in the west. For one thing, people aren't looking for people to have a short-term relationship with, but rather are seriously searching for a spouse. As such, there is no stigma to finding a spouse through a personal ad in a newspaper. The personal ads are sorted first of all by religion and then caste, since those are such important issues in marriage in India.

There is, however, also a section of ads for those looking for or open to inter-caste marriage. The ads often contain certain requirements for the potential spouse such as being a non drinker. They will also, of course, try to make themselves sound as good as possible. For instance, a woman may be advertised as being "homely," which in India does not mean unattractive, but rather domestic.

A woman may also be described as "wheatish" which means that she has lighter skin, which is often considered preferable. The potential groom will have his financial standing, if favorable, mentioned. If a family has ties to the royal family, the ad may say they are "well connected," which would be important to other families with a royal lineage.

If you happen to have a chance to get a newspaper while in India, do check out the classified ads for marriages for more insight into this way of finding a spouse. While you won't likely find a spouse for yourself there, it can make interesting reading!

Finding a spouse in India may seem complicated with unnecessary rules, but it has been working for generations and is unlikely to change drastically anytime soon.

The Significance of Nose Rings in Indian Culture

Nose rings may seem trendy in the West, but they have existed for centuries in many parts of the world and have stood the test of time in many countries, particularly India.

History of Nose Rings in India

Nose rings, although closely associated with Indian culture, actually originated in the Middle East. Nose rings first appeared in India during the Moghul period around the 16th century. In fact, excavations in India have not turned up any evidence of nose rings in India prior to the 16th century.

Types of Nose Rings in India

The nose rings that first appeared in India were not actual rings, but were small, flat, ornamental patterns - often flowers - that were held in place by a screw on the inside of the nostril.

The type of nose ring worn in India today is largely dependent on the area of the nose where the nose ring will be worn. For instance, studs, also known as phul, are common when worn in the nostril. Circular barbells, also known as nath, are worn in the septum (the cartilage between the nostrils), and straight barbells adorn the area on the bridge of the nose between the eyes. It's possible for septum rings to be so large that they make it difficult to eat.

Some nose rings are so heavily ornamented by jewels, pearls and so on, that chains, which are attached to the hair or over the earlobe are used to help support the weight of the nose ring.

Metals Used in Nose Rings in India

Most commonly nose rings in India are made out of 14 or 18 karat gold, but titanium, nickel, niobium, and stainless steel are also used.

Position of Nose Rings in India

As mentioned above in types of piercings, nose rings in India can be worn on the nostril, septum, or the bridge of the nose. However, most commonly, nose rings are worn on either the left or right nostril. Typically the left nostril is favored because in Ayurvedic medicine, the left nostril is associated with the female reproductive organs, and a piercing in that position is thought to make childbirth easier as well as lessen the amount of menstrual pain.

Nose Rings in India and Hinduism

Nose rings in India appear to be associated with Hinduism as they are worn by Hindu women more than by women of any other religion in India. However, it should be noted that Muslim women do also wear nose rings.

Connection of Nose Rings in India with Marriage

Many Indian women, particularly Hindus, have their noses pierced around the age of 16, which is traditionally the marriageable age. Piercings in India, including nose piercings, are one way Hindus honor Parvathi, the goddess of marriage.

In some parts of India the nose ring is never removed once a woman is married, and thus a nose ring is often considered to be a sign of marriage, even though today unmarried women and even young girls in India may also wear nose rings.
Holidays

Since Hinduism is the majority religion in India, many of the festivals in India are focused on various Hindu deities.

Since there are so many Hindu gods and goddesses, there are festivals happening all the time. In fact, I recall there being many times when I heard a racket outside and looked out my window to see some type of procession going on, in honor of a god that I perhaps was unfamiliar with, but who was very important the people celebrating at that particular time.

I'm only going to cover a few of the big festivals in India that I myself experienced, and then also cover a bit of my experience of celebrating American holidays in India.

Celebrating Holidays in India

One really important thing to keep in mind with Hindu festivals is that they are based on the lunar calendar, which means the dates for them change each year. In other words, while Christmas is celebrated every December 25, Diwali, for example, was celebrated on October 23 in 2014, but not until November 11, in 2015.

Because of that, if you want to be in India when a particular festival is celebrated, be sure to check for the dates the holiday will be celebrated during the year you plan to attend and book your flights to fit with the appropriate dates.

Diwali

In terms of Indian holidays, Diwali (also called Deepavali), referred to above was probably my favorite, because it reminded me of a cross between Christmas (due to the gift giving and lights) and the 4th of July (due to the fireworks).

Diwali is indeed known as the festival of lights. The lights are symbolic and represent the concept of light being victorious over darkness.

Diwali tends to be a happy time in India. People clean and decorate their homes in preparation for the holiday.

Diwali is also a great season for shopping, as people buy new clothing not just as gifts, but for themselves as well. Other popular gifts are appliances, and in some cases, even big ticket items such as cars.

Women and girls create rangoli, which are beautiful designs made with sand, as pictured at the top of this chapter. These designs are created on floors, in walkways, and near doors. Naturally, in the same way that sidewalk chalk doesn't last in the U.S., rangoli designs, while beautiful, are only temporary and can be messed up when people walk on them, and naturally wash away if it rains.

During Diwali you'll also see strings of lights everywhere, similar to how we see Christmas lights strung all over the place during the month of December.

You'll also hear fireworks going off all the time. Notice that I said "hear," rather than "see." I wrote hear without really thinking about it, and that gives you some indication of the noise level of the fireworks that people set off. Let's just say that I doubt most of the fireworks in India are legal anywhere in the U.S. as they are definitely powerful.

In addition to all shopping, lights, fireworks, and decorations, Diwali is a time when parents tell their children stories based on mythical battles between the forces of good and evil.

TRUE STORY

I have a few significant memories regarding celebrating Diwali in India.

One memory was the fun of giving our household help new clothing. I learned from some of my Indian friends that was a good thing to do, and it was great fun to see eyes light up when presenting expensive saris and other clothing items to people who worked for me.

Another was going from house to house of our friends, along with little boxes of sweets. This is a tradition the day after Diwali, when friends and family members visit each other and present gifts of sweets. We dropped by a lot of our friends' homes bearing sweets, and we were also visited by a lot of our friends with sweets in hand. The only downside to this was that I don't particular care for Indian sweets, and like it or not, I had to eat a lot of them the day after Diwali.

One thing that I was fortunate to experience that few foreigners likely do is to visit the Jodhpur palace and have brunch with the Maharaja the day after Diwali. One of my Indian friends was "well connected" to the Maharaja and arranged for my husband and I to go.

The interesting thing about this was that I saw first hand where culture and customs come in to play in such situations. First off, upon arrival, I ended up in a room full of women, as men and women were separated for this event, as is fairly common in India. We were all on our best behavior, dressed in our finest clothing, and rather quiet.

I'm not sure what I was expecting when I went, but quietly waiting wasn't it! Of course, at some point, the moment we were all waiting for -- the entrance of the Maharaja came. We all stood in respect, and many touched his feet.

In spite of being dressed in traditional Rajasthani dress, needless to say, I stood out in the crowd. I recall the Maharaja looking directly at me, as if to say, "What are YOU doing here?" We did have an opportunity to meet, but I can't say that any significant conversation took place.

One thing that struck me, however, is that later that week, I visited some friends and ran into some of the women who I had met at the place the day after Diwali. In the less formal setting, these women were relaxed, laughing, and having a good time, and I couldn't help but contrast their behavior that day with the quiet and respectful behavior that took place in the palace.

If it works with your schedule, even though you probably won't have a chance to meet a Raja, Diwali is a memorable time to visit India.

Holi

Holi is another big festival in India that I personally experienced. I hardly even know where to begin when it comes to describing Holi. Unlike Diwali, which reminded me of some of the holidays I celebrate in the U.S., there was no similar frame of reference for me when it comes to Holi. However, in recent years, Color runs are becoming popular in the Western world, and while I'm not certain of it, I wouldn't be at all surprised if color runs were started by someone who experienced Holi in India.

Holi is a time to celebrate the beginning of spring and the end of winter, and it's also a time that signifies the triumph of good over evil. It's a time to laugh, play, and generally have a good time.

An American friend of mine warned me to stay home on Holi, so I actually had no intention of getting involved in the madness, but when neighbors dropped by and invited us to "play Holi" we naturally obliged.

While I didn't enjoy Holi as much as I did Diwali, I'm glad that the neighbors invited us to get involved. I recall one of my female neighbors gently rubbing colored powder all over my face and she wished me a "Happy Holi." Children and adults a like engaged in tossing handfuls of colored powder at each other, and all around having a good time.

I'll admit that it tickled my funny bone to later that day stand up on my roof and overlook the street, and see rickshaw drivers and other people go by, with multi-colored clothing, hair and skin.

One thing that was not so funny was trying to get the dye washed out of my clothing, skin and hair. My clothing, including undergarments were permanently stained, and it took several days to wash the dye completely out of my hair, scalp, and skin.

Celebrating the Fourth of July in Jaipur, India

Probably the most memorable Fourth of July my family has ever celebrated happened in an unexpected place, Jaipur, India.

Although we were greatly enmeshed in Indian culture and life, holidays always left us feeling a bit nostalgic and homesick, so we did our best to celebrate American holidays while in India.

Once such holiday was the Fourth of July. Certain things such as apple pie was out, but knowing that watermelon was often consumed on the Fourth of July in the U.S., our wonderful cook, Chandu, prepared a special treat for us -- watermelon juice. We also picked up some Indian tandoori chicken from a nearby restaurant and some other special foods, though while different from what we'd eat in the U.S., were still good.

Lucky for us, India has fireworks. Lots and lots of fireworks. The fireworks in India are different from what you can buy in the U.S. in that from what I can tell, they are not in anyway regulated, so tend to be much more powerful than what we can buy in America.

We lived on the top floor of an apartment building, and had the entire flat, concrete roof, which was surrounded by a wall, all to ourselves. It was about 3,000 square feet large, so there was plenty of room for us to throw a big Fourth of July celebration for all of the Americans living in town, plus some close Indian friends.

We ate our delicious dinner and then all gathered around for the main event -- fireworks! We brought out boxes and boxes of fireworks that were sure to thrill all of our guests, and started lighting them. We were all having a great time, until we were all "thrilled" beyond what we anticipated.

We had saved an especially large firework for last, and had our faithful servant light it for us. We all gathered in a circle around it, in anticipation of what was sure to be a spectacular show of spinning fire.

It was spectacular, all right! Our servant had accidentally place it on the cement floor upside down before lighting it. The wrong position, coupled with the strong force of this particular firework caused the firework to explode with a loud bang, before it shot toward the crowd. All of our guests went running and screaming, trying to get away from it.

The entire thing was loud enough that all the other residents of the building ran outside, screaming, sure that a bomb had gone off. The building security guard did his best to assure everyone that it was just "the Americans celebrating a festival."

The next morning, when it was light, we walked onto the roof where we found a huge black mark, which is no doubt where the "bomb" went off. We quickly scrubbed the black mark off before our landlords came to visit us.

Although we've had many memorable Fourth of July celebrations before and since then, our family still fondly remembers the time we celebrated the Fourth of July in Jaipur, India in a way that everyone in the neighborhood still talks about.

Places to Stay, Things to Do

As I mentioned in the introduction, this isn't a traditional travel guide that lists numerous hotels and restaurants to stay in. For that, I recommend that you pick up a Lonely Planet guide for the specific region in India you plan to go.

However, I do want to share some tips based on my experience in India that I know you'll find helpful.

Delhi

Getting Around Delhi (and Other Cities in India)

During the time I spent in India, I learned a lot about getting around Indian cities. My biggest lessons have been learned through being ripped off, particularly by taxi and rickshaw drivers, but that doesn't mean those are bad ways to travel, as long as you know what you're doing. Below are the best ways to get around the city of Delhi, India, and tips for how to keep from being the victim of scams.

While this information is specific to Delhi, much of it applies to other cities in India as well.

Taxis

Taxis are a great way to get around the city of Delhi and chances are, if you arrive to Delhi by plane, as soon as you make it through customs, you'll be swarmed by Indian taxi drivers. As described in the Scams section of this book, my worst travel experience in India came through a taxi driver at the Delhi airport, but it could have been avoided if I kept the following tips in mind.

At the Delhi airport, be sure to arrange for a taxi to your hotel at one of the two Delhi Traffic Police Taxi Booths. One is inside the airport, and one is outside. The key is to make sure to go to a booth run by the police, rather than by independent taxi drivers. Under no circumstances should you agree to go with a taxi driver who approaches you directly.

A taxi ride from the Delhi airport to Paharganj should run you about 225 rupees, with a 25% surcharge between 11 p.m. and 5 a.m.

After paying at the prepaid taxi booth run by the police, you will receive a voucher with the address of your hotel. The voucher is how the taxi driver gets paid, so do not surrender the voucher to the taxi driver until he gets you safely to your hotel.

Getting Around Delhi, India in Rickshaws

Rickshaws are one of my favorite ways to get around Indian cities, in part because it's how the locals often travel. Auto-rickshaws are more common, but bicycle rickshaws are still used in Old Delhi. If you do have a chance to take a bicycle rickshaw, you should do it at least once for a unique experience that should only set you back about 15 rupees.

Auto-rickshaw rates around Delhi range between 30 and 80 rupees, depending on distance. Before leaving your hotel to go to a particular destination, ask at the hotel front desk how much it should cost to take an auto-rickshaw to your destination. Keep that amount in mind, when haggling over the fare with the rickshaw driver.

Do not get into the rickshaw until you have settled on a price. The rickshaw driver may say something like, "As you wish" when asked about the fare. Do not believe that he really means that you can pay whatever you want. Refuse to get into the rickshaw until a firm fare has been agreed on.

Buses in Delhi, India

If you really want to travel around Delhi like the locals, take a public bus, but be forewarned: Indian buses become very crowded and most do not have air conditioning. They are, however, very cheap. A bus trip won't set you back any more than 15 rupees, as long as you stay within the city limits. Short bus trips can cost as little as two rupees. I've also found that since few tourists take buses, many of the locals are happy to help make sure you get off at the right place, and there really aren't any scams to worry about.

Hot tip: Since Indian buses get so crowded, try to board the bus at the start of the route so you can get a seat.

Travel by Metro in Delhi

Hours of operation: 6 a.m. to 11 p.m.
www.delhimetrorail.com
phone: 24365204

The train is a great way to get around within the city of Delhi. Fares are reasonable, between 6 and 22 rupees. All departure announcements are in both Hindi and English, and tokens can be purchased for between 6 and 22 rupees. If you plan to use the metro extensively, the best option is to purchase a 1-day unlimited tourist card for approximately 70 rupees, or a three-day card for approximately 700 rupees.

Hot tip: If you're planning to stay in Delhi more than three days, for convenience sake, purchase a Smart Card for approximately 50 rupees. It can be recharged as needed, in amounts ranging from Rs50 to Rs800, and you won't have to mess with tokens.

Hired Car and Driver

If you want to avoid the stresses of multiple negotiations with rickshaw and taxi drivers throughout the time you are in Delhi, consider hiring a car and driver. This is the best way to have your own personal taxi to take you wherever you want to go.

The driver will take you to each of your destinations and wait for you while you see the sites. It is one of the safest ways to travel within the city of Delhi, but there are limits of a maximum of eight hours and 80 kilometers per day. The cost ranges between 700 rupees and 1100 rupees per day.

Hot tip: Be sure to use a reputable taxi company. The two listed below have been rated well by tourists.

Kumar Tourist Taxi Service

Phone: 23415930
kumartaxi@rediffmail.com
14/1 K-Block, Connaught Place, New Delhi, India
Metropole Tourist Service
Phone: 24310313
www.metrovista.co.in

224 Defence Colony Flyover Market (under the Defence Flyover Bridge, on the Jangpura side)

A Guide to Budget Hotels in New Delhi, India

Chances are, Delhi is the first city you'll land in in India, particularly if you plan to spend time in North India. In my experience, I've spent many nights in Delhi, before traveling to other cities in India. I wish I could say that all of my Delhi hotel experiences have been great, but unfortunately, I've had a couple that were downright scary. Budget hotels can be even more "memorable," particularly from a Western perspective, but that doesn't mean they have to be unsafe. Based on my own experience and research, here are some recommended budget hotels in New Delhi, India, that should do the job well enough if you're trying to tightwad your way through India.

Budget Hotels in the Paharganj Area of New Delhi, India

I personally kind of like the Paharganj area as a great place to shop, since there are multiple bazaars here. Another plus to Paharganj is that it is located very close to the New Delhi train station, so if you plan to travel from Delhi to another city in India by train, the Paharganj area is a great place to stay.

Hotel Downtown

4583 Main Bazaar
New Delhi, India
Telephone: 41541529

As to be expected with a budget hotel, the rooms at Hotel Downtown are small and very sparse, but they are clean and safe enough, and run around 300 rupees per night.

Hotel Rak International

Tooti Chowk, Main Bazaar
New Delhi, India
Telephone: 23562478

This is a budget hotel in the Paharganj area that actually has windows in the rooms. Windows are a plus or minus, depending on your perspective. As a plus, you'll have some natural sunlight to brighten your room and also be able to watch the street scene below for entertainment. The minus of a room in New Delhi that has windows is the noise, so you might want to pack some earplugs if you plan to stay here. This is slightly higher priced than Hotel Downtown at approximately 450 rupees per night.

Budget Hotels in the Connaught Place Area of New Delhi, India

Connaught Place is another popular spot in New Delhi that seems to be a little less harrowing than some other parts of Delhi. Particularly if you're not fond of Indian food, or at the very least might get a hankering for familiar food, Connaught Place is the place to be, since there are plenty of American chain restaurants located nearby.

Here are two budget hotels in the Connaught Place area of New Delhi, India:

Ringo Guest House

17 Scindia House, Connaught Lane
New Delhi, India

Telephone: 23310605
Email: ringo_guest_house@yahoo.co.in

Sunny Guest House

152 Scindia House, Connaught Lane
New Delhi, India
Telephone: 23312909
Email: sunnyguesthouse1234@hotmail.com

Both of these budget hotels located in the Connaught Place area of New Delhi run around 400 rupees per night, or about half that if you opt for a room without a bathroom. I'm not sure it's worth going without a bathroom just to save a couple of bucks a night, particularly with the tendency of Western travelers to get "Delhi belly," but for those about to head back home with barely enough money to get to the airport, opting for a room without a bathroom is a chance you might have to take.

A Guide to Moderately Priced Hotels in New Delhi, India

Some travelers to India love to see how little they can spend on hotels. You can indeed get quite a rush from spending less on an Indian hotel than you might spend at a fast-food restaurant in the U.S. Others want only the best, and opt to stay in luxury 5-star hotels, or perhaps even in an Indian palace that has been made into a hotel.

For the rest of us, the best option seems to be mid-range hotels, that are certainly reasonably priced by American standards, and comfortable enough for the average tourist. If you fit into the category of those who prefer moderately priced hotels, here are three of my recommended options in New Delhi.

A Recommended Mid-Range Hotel in Paharganj

Paharganj is located in a busy bazaar area in New Delhi. Because of that, it is a good place to stay if you like to shop. It's convenient because you can step right outside of your hotel and start shopping, and when your shopping bags start to get full, you can easily bring your finds back to your hotel room before heading out for more. It's also located close to the New Delhi train station, so if you're traveling by train to or from New Delhi, Paharganj is a convenient place to stay.

Metropolis Tourist Home

1634 Main Bazaar, Paharganj
New Delhi, India
Telephone: 23561794
www.metropolistravels.com

I have stayed in the Metropolis Tourist Home on a couple of my stays in New Delhi. The fact that I stayed there more than once indicates that it is an okay place to stay. A plus is that it has a good restaurant, which is not only convenient, but nice from a safety standpoint if you don't want to wander the streets of New Delhi after dark.

One negative thing about this particular location is that it has windows up near the ceiling of the bathroom, and when opened, it sounds like the people in the room next door are right inside of your room. My traveling companion and I awoke with a start one night because we thought someone was in our room due to the sound of someone coughing, as well as the smell of cigar smoke, both of which came from the room next door. Closing the window in the bathroom seems to remedy that problem.

The Metropolis Tourist Home will set you back roughly 1200 rupees per night.

A Recommended Mid-Range Hotel in the Connaught Place Area of New Delhi

Connaught Place is one of the nicer areas in New Delhi. Because of that, it is a generally pleasant and safe place to stay. It feels a bit more modern than a lot of parts of Delhi, and is home to many American chain restaurants, which is great if you're hankering for a taste of home.

YMCA Tourist Hostel

Jai Singh Road
New Delhi, India
Telephone: 23361915
Email: ymcath@ndf.vsnl.net.in

There's nothing fancy about this place, but it is clean and comfortable and in a great location. It also has a decent swimming pool, which is rare in mid-range hotels in India. Swimming costs around 200 rupees per person and the nightly tariff for the hotel is approximately 3500 rupees which includes breakfast and dinner.

A Recommended Mid-Range Hotel on Chanakyapuri and Ashoka Road in New Delhi, India

Though not as conveniently located as the two hotels mentioned above, this area is relatively quiet, and the streets are lined with trees. It takes about 20 minutes to get to Connaught Place by rickshaw from this area.

YWCA Blue Triangle Family Hostel

Ashoka Road
New Delhi, India
Telephone: 23360133
www.ywcaofdelhi.org
Though nothing fancy, I feel very safe when staying at the YWCA Blue Triangle. It is clean and comfortable, and the nightly tariff of approximately 2000 rupees and includes a simple but filling breakfast where both hot tea and coffee are served.

Each time I've stayed here, I had to dodge ants in the sugar bowl before spooning sugar into my coffee at the complimentary breakfast. While a bit disconcerting, such an experience is not unusual in India.

Luxury Hotels in New Delhi, India

I love India, but sometimes the stress of it wears me out. In those times, I find it helpful to pamper myself a bit by staying in a nice hotel, where I can relax after a long day of bargaining and fighting crowds. Generally speaking, beds in India are hard compared to what Westerners are used to, and sleeping in comfortable beds found in luxury hotels contribute significantly to an overall feeling of energy and well-being. Here are a few recommend luxury hotels in New Delhi, India.

A Great Place to Stay in New Delhi, After the Long International Flight

One of the most exhausting things about India is simply getting there. In most of my trips to India, I've traveled for at least 30 hours, including layovers, before finally touching down in Delhi. Even worse, it seems that flights to Delhi typically arrive around midnight, with it being around 1 a.m. before making it through customs and picking up luggage. By then, most travelers are extremely weary and in need of a good night's sleep. To hasten this process, try staying in a hotel near the airport. Here's one I would recommend:

Radisson Hotel, New Delhi

National Highway 8
Telephone: 26779191
www.radisson.com/newdelhiin

As can be expected with an American hotel chain, you can expect American comfort - and prices - at the Radisson Hotel near the New Delhi airport. Priced at approximately $375 USD per night, the Radisson has comfortable beds, and Chinese, Italian and kebab restaurants.

Other Luxury Hotels in New Delhi, India

Staying near the airport is great when first arriving to or departing from India, but for the rest of your stay in Delhi, you might want to opt for something with a bit more of an Indian feel to it. A great choice is the Taj Mahal Hotel.

Taj Mahal Hotel in New Delhi, India

Man Singh Road
Telephone: 23026162
www.tajhotels.com

The Taj Mahal hotel does a great job of creating an exotic Indian atmosphere by decorating with Persian rugs and Indian artwork. Expect to pay approximately $400 USD per night for amenities such as luxurious bathrooms, electronic safes, a full mini-bar, complimentary transportation from the airport, butler service, and breakfast served in the lounge.

Shangri-La Hotel

19 Ashoka Road
Connaught Place
New Delhi 110 001, India

Telephone: 4119 1919
www.shangri-la.com

The Shangri-La Hotel is constructed in such a way that those who wanted to avoid the traffic and other headache that are part of life in New Delhi can do so if desired. With a variety of restaurants, and even an art gallery, everything you need is provided for you without ever needing to leave the hotel. However, guests who do decide to venture out can arrange a tour of the city with the concierge. These tours are provided in style in cars such as the Rolls Royce Phantom. This hotel is priced at around $400 USD per night.

Going to India doesn't mean you have to rough it. Staying in a luxury hotel is a great way to experience the best of India while avoiding some of the less pleasant aspects of life in India.

Rajasthan

The name, "Rajasthan" literally means, "Land of the Kings." As you probably guessed, this is where the word, "Rajas" in the title of this book came from.

There are still rajas (more appropriately called, "maharajas" which means, "high king") in India today. Each major city in Rajasthan has a palace, fort, and of course, maharajah. So if you want to experience the royal side of India, Rajasthan is the place to go!

Rajasthan Homestays

Unless you're dead set on staying in hotels, on your visit to Rajasthan, I recommend that you instead consider the "homestay" option. Homestays are similar to the bed and breakfast inns we have in the U.S. in that they are larger homes that have been converted into a small hotel of sorts. While there are private rooms, there are also common areas such as living areas, courtyards, and dining rooms, where guests may eat together.

The great thing about it is that you can make all of your Rajasthan homestay arrangements through Rajputana Discovery.

This company is owned by Chandrashekhar and Bhavna Singh, a couple that I met and got to know quite well when I lived in Jodhpur.

When I returned to India for a visit with a friend of mine, during our time in Jodhpur, I stayed at Indrashan, which was the homestay location in Jodhpur. The great thing about this is that this gave me an opportunity to experience their homestay as tourists do, since I stayed in the rooms, had my meals there, and so on, instead of just dropping by for a visit as I did when I lived in Jodhpur.

In addition to being a safe and quiet location, the food was excellent, the rooms were clean and comfortable, and the showers had good water pressure -- which is not something to be taken for granted in India.

I also enjoyed sharing meals with other tourists, from all over the world. One thing I observed was the great care that Chandrashekhar and Bhavna provided to make sure guests had everything they needed, whether that was more chai, or transportation to a local spice shop they recommended.

At the current time, prices range from 1,940 rupees to 2,750 rupees per night with a hot, homemade breakfast costing 225, lunch 450 and dinner 555. Meals are optional, and you can pick and choose which meals, if any, you want to eat there.

The homestays in other cities in Rajasthan are run by people personally known by, and in some cases related to, Chandrashekhar and Bhavna. I haven't stayed in any of them, but knowing the type of people the Singhs are, don't hesitate at all to recommend them.

You can connect with them via their website at http://rajputanadiscovery.com.

A Guide to the Forts of Rajasthan, India

One of my favorite things in Rajasthan is the rich architecture, particularly the forts and palaces. From my rooftop in Jodhpur and from almost anywhere else in the city for that matter, I could look up and see the magnificent Mehrangarh Fort. I'll never forget my first trip there, and the way that walking through the halls of a building unlike any we have in the United States ignited my imagination.

If you want to take a step back in time and dream about princely battles and opulent lifestyles, be sure to visit the forts of Rajasthan the next time you go to India. Below is a list of some of the forts in Rajasthan that you don't want to miss.

The Fort in Jodhpur, India

Mehrangarh Fort
Fort Road
Open daily from 9 a.m. to 5 p.m.
Telephone: 291-254-8790
www.mehrangarh.org

Mehrangarh Fort in Jodhpur, is truly one of the most majestic forts in all of India. Founded in 1450 by Rao Jodha and added to be later maharajas until its completion in the 19th century, sits atop a 400-foot high hill. The fort houses a museum that displays artifacts of Indian royalty. There is also a nice selection of Indian miniature paintings available for sale.

Amber Fort in Jaipur, India

There are actually three forts in Jaipur, but Amber Fort is one of my favorites and the favorite of many tourists as well. The Amber Fort is one of the better places in India to have an opportunity to take a ride on a brightly decorated elephant. In fact, Amber Fort was the first place I ever rode an elephant.

The construction of Amber Fort began in 1592 and took 125 years to complete. The art and architecture of Amber Fort combines both Rajput and Moghul influences.

Amber Fort Location

Amber Fort is actually located 11 kilometers (7 miles) north of Jaipur, but any rickshaw or taxi driver can easily get you there.

Hours of operation: Open daily from 9 a.m. - 4:30 p.m.
Telephone: 0141-253-0293

When you visit the forts in Rajasthan, plan to also visit palaces that are typically located very close to the fort. Some of the palaces have been converted into luxury hotels, so if your pocketbook permits, you might want spend a day touring a fort and then spend the night in the luxury of an Indian palace right next door.

If you want a taste of royalty but can't quite afford a night in a palace, try making dinner reservations at a palace. My husband and I celebrated an unforgettable wedding anniversary on the terrace of the palace in Jodphur. The food was better than any I've had in India, we were served by waiters wearing Indian formal wear, including formal turbans and we had a beautiful view of the city lights as dusk turned to night.

Jodhpur

Jodhpur was the first Indian city I called home. I suppose the fact that I fell in love with many aspects of India in Jodhpur contributes to my love for the city, even though it isn't the top tourist destination in India. In spite of other Indian cities being more popular, Jodhpur has some magnificent sites to visit, and the fact that it moves at a slower pace than much of India makes it a great place to spend a couple of days.

It only takes about five hours to go by train from Jaipur to Jodhpur, so consider adding Jodhpur to your itinerary if you plan to visit Jaipur. Read on for a few of my favorite things to do in Jodhpur, India.

Mehrangarh Fort

No trip to North India is complete without visiting the forts of Rajasthan, as mentioned above. Mehrangarh Fort is one of the best forts in India. Part of the magnificence of Mehrangarh Fort is the fact that it sits atop a 410 foot high sheer rock cliff and can be seen for miles. One of my favorite rooms in the fort is the Phool Mahal, a gilded room with intricate paintings that was built over a 20-year span between 1730 and 1750. This room was used for royal celebrations.

The Moti Mahal was built in the 1500s, over a period of 14 years. This is a room that literally shines due to the mirror work on the ceilings as well as crushed shells that were mixed into the plaster on the walls to give the room a luxurious sheen. This room was used by the maharajah as a private audience hall.

Umaid Bhavan Palace

Open daily from 9 a.m. to 5 p.m.
Telephone: 0291-251-0101

I have especially fond memories of the Umaid Bhavan Palace in Jodhpur since my husband and I celebrated our 14th anniversary there. We enjoyed dinner sitting on the terrace, overlooking the city at night. In addition to dinner options, the palace is also open for tours, and you can even book a room in the luxurious hotel that is part of the palace.

Lassi at the Clock Tower

Downtown Jodhpur has a clock tower that can't be missed. Sadar Bazaar, located near the clock tower, is a great place to shop, so be sure to check it out on your trip to Jodhpur.

Even more impressive than the bazaar is an unassuming restaurant, with a spectacular yogurt drink, the lassi. The lassi shop located at the clock tower in Jodhpur serves lassis that are far better than any other I've had anywhere in India.

They are so thick, you can stand your spoon up in the middle of the lassi. This lassi shop, unknown to a lot of tourists, is a favorite of locals. Even if you don't think you like lassis, give the ones at the clock tower a try. I doubt you'll be disappointed.

Romantic Travel Destinations in North India

North India is a land of exotic forts and palaces. The Mughul architecture there immediately transports visitors to a different time and place, where they can't help but feel nostalgic and romantic. Because of that, it is a great place to head for a destination wedding, or for a second honeymoon, or to add a touch or romance to your India travels, regardless of why you're there.

Here are my top picks for romantic travel destinations in North India.

Jaisalmer

Jaisalmer is a city that looks straight out of a medieval storybook. As is the case with many of the locations in North India, it has its share of breathtaking architecture, with the majority of the older buildings constructed out of sandstone.

Although the Jaisalmer Fort may seem to be an ideal and romantic place the stay, due to poor drainage, the fort is crumbling, and therefore may not be the best place to stay. Instead, consider staying at The Searai, a luxury tented camp and spa:

The Serai

Bherwa,
Chandan,
District Jaisalmer,
Rajasthan 345 001
India
Telephone: (+91) (11) 4606 7608

reservations@sujanluxury.com
http://www.the-serai.com/the_serai.html

Rathambore

Rathambore is an excellent romantic North India travel destination, particularly for wildlife lovers. The Rathambore National Park is one of the best places in India to spot a tiger. It is also a place filled with history, where tales of valor inspire dreams of what it may have been like to live in days gone by.

Although there is a luxurious tent lodging option at Amani-I-Khas, at a price of nearly $1000 per night, it is no doubt beyond the budgets of many. A more affordable option in the same area is the Khem Villas, a luxury jungle resort, where lodging prices hover around a more affordable $200 per night.

Kehm Villas

VPO Sherpur Khiljipur, Dist. Sawai Madhopur, Rajasthan, INDIA
Telephones: 094140 30262, 07462 252347, 07462 252348
E-mail: khemvillas@anokhi.com
http://www.khemvillas.com/

Udaipur

Udaipur is undoubtedly one of the most romantic cities in all of India, known for its lake palace. Since Udaipur is a city of palaces, it makes perfect sense to stay in a palace for your special event, whether it be a honeymoon, or simply a romantic getaway with the person you love.

If your budget permits it, the Taj Lake Palace is my pick for the most romantic lodging option in Udaipur. Situated on Lake

Pichola, not only are the rooms luxurious, the views of the lake cannot be beat.

Taj Lake Palace

P.O. Box 5, Lake Pichola
Udaipur - 313001
Rajasthan, India
Telephone: +91 294 2428800
Facsimile: (0294) 2428700
http://www.tajhotels.com/Luxury/Grand-Palaces-And-Iconic-Hotels

How to Enjoy a Visit to Pushkar, India

One of the most fascinating experiences I ever had in India was a visit to Pushkar. At the time I had already been in India for a few months, and I thought I had seen it all, but I saw and experienced things in Pushkar that I have never seen or experienced anywhere else. Pushkar can be either a great or horrible experience, depending on when you go and whether or not you're prepared for what you'll encounter. This chapter will help you know what to expect and how to make sure that your visit to Pushkar is an enjoyable one.

Understand the Sacred Nature of Pushkar

Pushkar is believed to be one of the holiest cities in India due to the belief that it was formed when Lord Brahma dropped a lotus flower to earth. Because of this, there are over 500 temples in this small town, and 52 ghats that lead into Pushkar Lake, where

Hindu pilgrims go to bathe, since they believe by doing so, their sins will be washed away. Due to the religious nature of the city, many of the attractions focus on the Hindu religion, with a main attraction being the Brahma temple.

Go to Pushkar the Right Time of Year

You can go to Pushkar any time of year and enjoy it, but the time of year you go will greatly impact the ins and outs of your visit. If you prefer a quiet, sleepy town, it's best to go between December and September, though the summer months should be avoided due to heat, if at all possible.

If, however, you like lots of crowds and action, and the opportunity to observe everything from snake charmers, musicians, magicians, and children balancing on high poles, not to mention numerous shows put on by transvestites (known as eunuchs), you'll want to go during the annual camel festival, which takes place in either October or November of each year.

As is true with all Hindu festivals, the dates of the festival are based on the lunar calendar, so they are different each year. If you don't want to miss it, be sure to check the dates of the camel festival before you go.

Prepare for Crowds

If you decide to go to Pushkar for the camel festival and other religious activities taking place the same week, be prepared for huge crowds. Pushkar generally has a population of around 13,000, but during the camel festival, the number of people in town swells to around 200,000.

The crowds are so bad that no matter how diligent my friend and I were in trying to stick together, we found it impossible to walk side by side and lost each other numerous times.

There is absolutely no space between people, so you also cannot easily stop to look at something, as the crowds push you along the road. Due to the large crowds and the intensity of the festival and all of the religious happenings, it is best not to bring children to Pushkar during the camel festival.

Book Your Room in Pushkar Several Weeks in Advance

As you can imagine, when a population of 13,000 swells to 200,000 in a single week, lodging is sparse, and many of the accommodations in the city are subpar. If you want to stay in a decent and safe place, book your lodging as soon as you book your plane tickets, or even before, if you're sure you're going.

My friend and I were not so lucky (or smart), and we had what I would call an "unforgettable" hotel experience. Here's the short version:

We were 100% exhausted when we arrived, so I wanted nothing more than to hit the sack as soon as we got to our room. However, when checked into our room, we noticed there was only ONE SMALL towel (about the size of a typical kitchen towel). My friend quipped, "Maybe they thought we could share the towel since it's so big."

While funny, the towel situation needed to be rectified, so we went to the front desk to ask for another towel. We also noticed there was no soap, so we asked for that as well.

Apparently our request, though seemingly normal to us, was quite challenging, and it took about 45 minutes to get them.

By that point, we were beyond tired, and so upon arriving back to our room, got ready for bed. Finally, ready to slip into the tiny twin-sized bed, I pulled the "top" sheet forward, only to find out that there was no bottom sheet. And there was no blanket.And the mattress looked filthy.

Not wanting to lay directly on the mattress, I folded the one sheet in half, so that I could use it as both a top and bottom sheet, got into bed and rolled myself into a little ball, to fit inside the tiny folded sheet. That's when I realized how cold it was.

Spurred on by another burst of ingenuity, I got up, pulled some clean clothes out of my suitcase, and laid them over me to help keep me warm.

Unfortunately, the bathroom situation was even worse than the bed situation, with there being no mirror, no hot water, and a hole in the floor for a toilet. (And no, I'm not talking about a typical Indian squatty potty, but a roughly hewn hole in the plywood floor.)

Needless to say, we survived the situation, and it gave me a good story to tell, but if I had it to do over again, I'd make arrangements FAR in advance!

The Royal Safari Camp

So you've heard about one of the worst places to stay, now let's take a look at one of the best places to stay in Pushkar during the camel festival-- the Royal Safari Camp. Don't let the fact that the rooms are tents fool you. They are by far the nicest place to stay in Pushkar, with 20 of the 60 tents having air conditioning. The tents have private bathrooms with western-style toilets, and the guests are served delicious and safe-to-eat meals. There are even luxuries such as toilet paper that are missing in many of the hotels in Pushkar.

India Camel Safari Tips

One of the best things about international travel is that it provides the opportunity to do things you would never do at home. One of my fondest India travel memories is of a camel safari in Rajasthan.

Riding a camel was far different than I imagined it would be, and in fact, I came very close to falling face forward into the sand the first time I tried it. Here are a few tips for how to make the most out of your India camel safari.

Choose a Reputable Camel Safari Guide

Think about it: on a camel safari, you're going to be far away from populated areas, out in the middle of the desert. You want to be sure that the camel safari guide you choose is reputable and dependable.

Lonely Planet recommends Camel Man in Bikaner and Trotters in Jaisalmer. Assuming you are staying in a reputable hotel or guest house, you can also depend on the owners to make arrangements with a good safari guide.

My friends from Rajputana Discovery that I mentioned earlier can also help you with this.

Hold on Tight

On my first camel ride, I felt relaxed and confident. When my camel guide said, "Hold on," I lightly put my hands on a metal ring on the saddle. He then, very emphatically said, "No, hold on tight." I'm glad I listened. As the camel began to stand, I was immediately thrust forward, and almost fell face first into the sand, in spite of the fact that I was holding on tight.

Since then, I've learned that in addition to holding on tight, it is a good idea to do the opposite of what the camel does. For instance, when the camel begins to stand up and move face down, lean back, as far as you can. By leaning back, you balance out the forward motion of the camel, and don't have the problem of almost falling off.

As the camel moves into a more upright position, you can sit straight up. Once the camel is standing all the way up, you can relax, and even have your hands free to do things such as photography.

Wear Proper Clothing

Long pants are ideal for a camel ride, since they help protect your legs from the rough fur of the camel. Flip flops or sandals are fine to wear, as long as there are stirrups. To be on the safe side, either wear sandals with heel straps, or wear shoes that are enclosed. Since you will be out in the hot desert sun, it is also advisable to wear a hat, and a lightweight, loose fitting, long-sleeved shirt or blouse to protect yourself from the sun.

Keoladeo National Park and Chandra Mahal Haveli

If you're a bird lover, and you have an opportunity to do so, be sure to check out the Keoladeo National Park http://keoladeonationalpark.com/, formerly known as the Bharatpur Bird Sanctuary. It's located between Jaipur and Agra, so an excellent plan is to spend time in Jaipur, visiting the fabulous forts and palaces, and then hire a car and driver to take you from Jaipur to Agra, stopping at the bird sanctuary along the way.

It is definitely off the beaten path, so you won't have nearly as many options for places to stay in that area. The great news is that there is a fabulous Haveli (mansion) that has been turned into a hotel that is nearby the bird sanctuary.

I would definitely recommend that you stay at the Chandra Mahal Haveli http://www.amritara.co.in/bharatpur/chandra-mahal-haveli.html. It's very different from any other place you will stay, as it is in the middle of a village. It was built in 1840, so is obviously very old, but it has been well maintained.

When my friend and I arrived, they fired up the generators, and had a delicious meal prepared for us in no time. It was missing some of the modern amenities that we are all used to, such as WiFi. Also, I went there in the winter and it was quite cold, but in spite of not having in-room heating, they took care of us just fine; they provided us hot water bottles to keep us warm while we slept. That was a first for me, but it worked!

Masala (Mixture)

The word, "masala" means mixture. And in this section I include a hodgepodge of topics that aren't large enough to warrant their own section.

Coping with Poverty

One thing that you'll encounter in India that you're probably not overly accustomed to is poverty. Lots and lots of poverty. We do see this some in the western world nowadays in the form of homelessness, but it's nothing like what you'll see in India.

This is an unsettling experience for most foreigners, as it should be. While being "unsettled" about something like this is a good thing, it's also important to know how to cope with it.

The natural inclination is to hand money to beggars when approached, and while that may be the natural inclination, it's not always the best. The reason is that often when you do so, you'll end up being descended upon by a huge crowd that seems to come from nowhere.

One thing you can do, however, is to give from inside of a taxi, if you'd like to. It will not be uncommon to have your taxi approached by beggars when the car stops, and many times they may bang on your window. That can be unsettling, for sure, and you can respond to it in a couple of ways. You can "ignore" it --

which is near impossible, or you can roll down your window and give some money.

The best thing about this is that you do at least have some buffer from inside your car, and if your car is swarmed after you give one beggar money, you can at least roll up the window. This seems so cold hearted, I know, and I struggle with it a lot, but there is truly no end to people approaching you for money while you're in India, and so you do need a buffer.

TRUE STORY

To give you some idea of what the swarm mentality can look like, I'd like to relate one of our giving stories. Our family went to McDonalds one night for dinner. From our table, we saw two little girls who were clearly beggars, looking in at us while we ate. My husband decided that when we finished eating, he would buy two Happy Meals to give these little girls.

After eating, he stepped outside to give the girls their meals, and no joke, from out of nowhere, around 30 children ascended on us and started grabbing at the Happy Meals. French fries flew everywhere, as my husband tried to regain control of the situation. Let's just say it wasn't one of our most fond memories of India.

Now having said that, food is a good thing to give to people, and if you have a backpack or fairly large bag or purse with you, you can carry some fruit, and packaged food items that you can pick up a local India markets. Providing food like this can often be more preferable than giving money, because sometime beggars, especially children, work for someone else, and aren't able to keep the money given to them, but can eat food given to them.

If you are there longer term, you'll have more of a struggle with this one, as there is a limit to how much you can give. Because of this, you'll definitely need to pick and choose who to give to. I recall one day when I was walking up the street in my neighborhood; I was approached by beggars -- a man pushing a woman who had no legs, on a cart. I walked passed them without giving anything, and as I did, the Bible verse, "Blessed is he who considers the poor. The Lord will deliver him in time of trouble" (Psalm 41:1) came to mind. At that moment, I knew that I was supposed to give. I stopped in my tracks, pulled a larger than normal "donation" out of my wallet and went back and gave to them. You may not have such a clear prompting, but I can say that if you are there longer term, you will need to pick and choose who to give to.

Ugly American

One of the most embarrassing and irritating things for me when in India is to see the arrogant behavior of my fellow Americans.

If you're an American (or perhaps from another western country), let me implore you -- don't be the ugly American.

If you want things to be "just like they are at home," then stay home. The bottom line is that things in India won't be like they are in the U.S. Service may be slower. Actually, I can almost guarantee that it will be slower. So slow down, and enjoy your meal, rather than getting annoyed when it takes longer to get your goods, or your check.

You'll also experience hearing the words, "not available" when you order something in a restaurant. Yes, this is frustrating, especially if it took you a long time to figure out what you want to eat, then have to wait a long time to have your order taken, only to find out that what you want isn't available. Keep in mind that there may be many reasons why something on the menu isn't available, and getting mad about it won't help.

At any rate, when packing your bags, be sure to pack an extra dose of patience, because you'll likely need it when in India. Choose not to be demanding, but instead, be pleasant and kind, even when things don't go your way.

Visas and Other Legal Issues

The first thing that you need to keep in mind is that you will need both a passport and a visa to visit India. You first need to get your passport, and then your visa, and both can take around six weeks, so don't dilly dally when it comes to taking care of this boring but necessary aspect of your travel prep.

If you have procrastinated, and need to get your passport in a hurry, try going to a passport agency near you. Just do a Google search for, "Passport agency [name of city]." Most likely you will only have this option if you are in a large city or don't mind traveling to one.

If you're an American and either in a hurry, don't live near a passport agency, or just don't want to deal with this on your own, then I'd recommend Travel Docs http://www.traveldocs.com/. Travel docs can help you get both a passport and a visa fast -- for a price.

Even if you want to do everything yourself and save yourself some cash, Travel Docs is a great site to check out because it has a lot of good information on what you need to do to get a visa. For example, this page http://www.traveldocs.com/index.php?page=india-tourist-visa-houston provides helpful information regarding what is needed, such as a passport that doesn't expire within six months and has at least two blank pages.

If you're from a country other than the U.S. or simply want to do everything on your own, here is where you need to start: https://indianvisaonline.gov.in/. This is actually where I've gone to take care of my own visas, as I didn't mind working through the paperwork and wanted to save some cash, especially since our whole family was going.

The standard tourist visa is good for six months, so while you want to do things in advance, you don't want to do them so far in advance that your visa expires before your trip!

If you think you'll make multiple trips to India, then a great option is to apply for a 10-year, multiple-entry tourist visa. This doesn't mean that you can stay in India for 10 years straight; you can still only stay for a maximum of six months at a time. But the great thing about this is that you won't have to reapply for visas for future trips, until the visa expires 10 years down the road. I actually got a 10-year visa, and it saved me not only money, but a lot of headaches since I only had to apply for one visa for the four trips I took to India.

One word of caution on this is that the Indian government may be less likely to approve your application for a 10-year multiple-entry visa, so if you choose to go this route, be sure to allow a bit of extra time in case your application is denied, and you have to reapply for a shorter visa.

Staying Connected

Fortunately, it's now easier than ever to stay connected to the rest of the world when you're in India. Chances are, if you stay in one of the nicer hotels, they'll have WiFi. If your hotel doesn't have WiFi, simply ask at the front desk for the nearest Internet café. These are becoming so common that unless your off the beaten path, you won't even have to try very hard to find one.

You can also check with your cell phone carrier to see if they have International service, and enable it before you leave for your trip. Needless to say, this tends to be a pricy option, but it can be worth it for the sake of convenience, if you want to have an easy way to stay connected with friends and family back home. This is probably the best option if you're going to India and your spouse and/or children are staying home.

Packing List

Before you go on any trip, it's a good idea to create a packing list, but this is even more true before going to India, as you may not be able to get some of the things you want. Even if you can find everything you may want, why be bothered with trying to find it?

Now having said that, it's best to travel as light as possible, since it can be a hassle to lug your luggage all over the place.

Here are a few things to add to your regular packing list:

Modest clothing. Women travelers need to avoid tight pants, shorts, capris, sleeveless tops, etc. While not as big of a concern for men, men should still avoid shorts and tank tops. It's fine to pack less modest clothing if you plan to wear it only in your hotel room, but don't run out in public in it, even for a few minutes.

Money belt or travel wallet. If you wear a belt anyway, you may as well make it a money belt, as a way of keeping your money safe. I personally like using a travel wallet that has a long, thin strap so I can hang the wallet around my neck and tuck it under my blouse. This is a great option because it enables you to keep your passport, plane ticket and other paperwork, and money safe, in a hands free way.

Medication. In addition to any prescription medication you need, pack anti-diarrheal -- Pepto tablets, cold or cough medicine, and something for headaches. You can buy many of these items in country, but again, why go through the hassle, especially since medications take very little room.

Sun block. This is really only needed if you're going to be outside a lot, but chances are, you will, even if you're in the city.

Water purification items. You should definitely plan to buy bottled water when in India, but it won't hurt to have water purification tablets or a high quality small water filter with you, "just in case."

Passport. You're not going to get very far without your passport. Your visa will be attached to the inside of your passport, so other than remembering to apply for your visa in plenty of time, you don't have to worry about packing it.

Travel insurance information. There's no point in applying for travel insurance, if you don't take the information with you. While you may be able to access the information online, it's best to have paper copies with you. The last thing you need when under the stress of an emergency is to have to try to obtain the information online.

Extra copies of important paperwork. Just in case your passport gets lost or stolen, you want to make sure to have a copy of it. If you're traveling with a companion, give copies to them as well, just in case a bag is stolen. This is also true for all other important paperwork such as copies of travelers checks.

Basic first aid items such as bandages, antiseptics, etc.

Laundry items. You can definitely have your laundry done inexpensively in India, but it may not get done on time, which can really cause a big problem. Because of this, I find it helpful to carry a small bottle of laundry detergent. If you can't find a very small, travel size bottle of laundry detergent, purchase a small bottle and fill it with detergent. You'll also want to pack a large, flat rubber sink stopper that will fit over any size drain, and 2-3 plastic hangers that you can use to hang up clothes to drip dry. Obviously, it can take a while for clothes to dry, so if you choose to do some of your own laundry, be sure to wash it early in the morning the day before you're moving on, so it has plenty of time to dry.

Female urinary device - optional

http://www.shalusharma.com/essential-travel-items-for-india/

Pack important papers, medication, and at least one change of clothes in carry on bag in case your other luggage gets lost.

Recommended Resources

I hope that you've enjoyed thoughts from my journey to India, and even more importantly that it will help you go on your own fantastic journey.

If you need more assistance in planning your trip, I'd like to recommend that you check out books by Shalu Sharma and that you contact my friends at Rajputana Discovery. I know that both things will help make your trip to India be an unforgettable experience!

Please Leave a Review

If you enjoyed this book, please leave a review on Amazon. Reviews encourage others to buy the book, so they really help! To leave a review go to:

https://www.amazon.com/review/create-review/ref=cm_cr_dp_wrt_summary?ie=UTF8&asin=B00SKIPLQM

91630079R00102

Made in the USA
Middletown, DE
01 October 2018